W9-DFS-154

 DESIGN FOR SPECIAL EVENTS

First published in the United States of America by
Rockport Publishers, a member of
Quayside Publishing Group
100 Cummings Center
Suite 406-L
Beverly, Massachusetts 01915-6101
Telephone: (978) 282-9590
Fax: (978) 283-2742
www.rockpub.com

Library of Congress Cataloging-in-Publication Data

Top Design Studio (Los Angeles, Calif.)
  Design for special events : 500 of the best event logos, invitations, and graphics / Top Design.
     p. cm.
  Includes index.
  ISBN 1-59253-400-7
  1. Commercial art--Catalogs. 2. Graphic arts--Catalogs. 3. Special events--Marketing. I. Title.
  NC997.T67 2008
  741.6--dc22

                                                          2007044060

ISBN-13: 978-1-59253-400-5
ISBN-10: 1-59253-400-7

10 9 8 7 6 5 4 3 2 1

Book Concept: Peleg Top
Design and Production: Top Design

Printed in China

BEVERLY MASSACHUSETTS

DESIGN FOR SPECIAL EVENTS

500 OF THE BEST LOGOS, INVITATIONS, AND GRAPHICS

PRESENTED BY TOP DESIGN, LOS ANGELES (topdesign.com)

ROCKPORT PUBLISHERS

CONTENTS

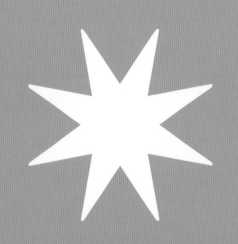

ABOUT THE AUTHOR

Peleg Top is principal and founder of Top Design, a Los Angeles–based studio specializing in design for special events. Founded in 1991, the studio has a rich portfolio of design and branding work for an array of distinguished clients.

With roots in the entertainment and nonprofit sectors, Top Design has worked with notable industry leaders such as the Grammys, City of Hope, Tiger Woods Foundation, and Toyota.

Top Design has been featured in such major design publications as *Print*, *HOW*, and *Communication Arts* and has received numerous awards for design excellence.

Author of *Letterhead & Logo Design* (Rockport Publishers, 2003), Top Design is known for clean, simple, and sophisticated work. It brings a strong history of successful design and branding experience to the event-planning arena.

INTRODUCTION

As a studio focused on design for special events, we often look for sources of creative inspiration, but had difficulty finding books showcasing incredible invitations, spot-on promotions, or other outstanding designs for events. So we decided to write our own.

The process of putting this book together was full of pleasant surprises. After we issued a call for submissions, we were thrilled by the response from the design community and the number of projects we received. In this generation of electronic invitations, we were at first shocked and then encouraged to see that print is still alive and well in the special event industry. We were impressed by the obvious care, inventiveness, and the high production values exhibited in many of these pieces.

Creative professionals recognize that designing for special events is a distinct discipline because its designs are inherently short lived, generally seen only for the duration of the event, and then never seen again. Because it doesn't need to stand the test of time, the work can be completely of the moment. This ephemeral nature affords the designer the freedom to take risks, to be innovative and creative—the qualities we specifically wanted to include in this book.

While most graphic design aims to promote a company or product, special event design promotes a singular experience. Special event designers need to capture the mood and excitement surrounding the event, even before it begins, by creating a promotional piece that evokes those emotions while identifying what makes the event memorable or unique. The initial project—a save-the-date mailer, an invitation or a promotional poster—must make the guest eager to attend. When we were judging submissions for this book, we looked for this engaging quality, asking about each piece, "Does this make us want to attend?"

In sifting through the nearly 1,500 submitted pieces, we were struck by the overall quality of the work and by the variety of events represented. We saw designs for everything from benefits to elaborate sporting events, to film festivals, and weddings, and a myriad of other types of gatherings. We were especially surprised at the number of beautifully designed fund-raising and nonprofit pieces received and were thoroughly impressed with how designers were able to meet the difficult challenge of promoting a cause that affects people in a personal (and often tragic) way, while capturing the fun and positive nature of a fund-raiser.

In organizing all of these projects, we found that everything fit into one of eight categories: fund-raising, entertainment, sports and automotive, community and education, business, awards, art and design, and private parties.

Among the 500 exceptional designs that we compiled to create this book, we've singled out nineteen events for case studies. The selected pieces either showed the seamless evolution of design in multiyear events or involved elaborate systems that were carried through an entire event, from invitations to signage and elements of the décor. Each of these nineteen case studies represents a unique special occasion, a serious fund-raiser, an energetic sporting event, or an exciting music festival for which each designer perfectly captured a mood and sentiment.

The quality and scope of event designs that we discovered while creating this book were both eye opening and encouraging. We hope you have a similar experience as you flip through the pages.

1 |
EVENT   29th Annual Festival Ball
CLIENT   City of Hope

2 |
EVENT   Humanity through Technology
CLIENT   The Shoah Foundation

1

Northern California Food & Drug Industries Circle

29th Annual

Festival Ball

SATURDAY, SEPTEMBER 8, 2007
Westin St. Francis Hotel | San Francisco

City of Hope

2

AN INVITATION

HUMANITY *through* TECHNOLOGY

teach

TRANSFORMING THE WAY HISTORY IS TAUGHT AND LEARNED

1 |

EVENT   26th Annual Festival Ball
CLIENT   City of Hope

2 |

EVENT   24th Annual Festival Ball
CLIENT   City of Hope

1

1 |

EVENT   40th Grammy Awards

CLIENT   The Recording Academy

2 |

EVENT   MusiCares Person of the Year

CLIENT   Musicares Foundation

2

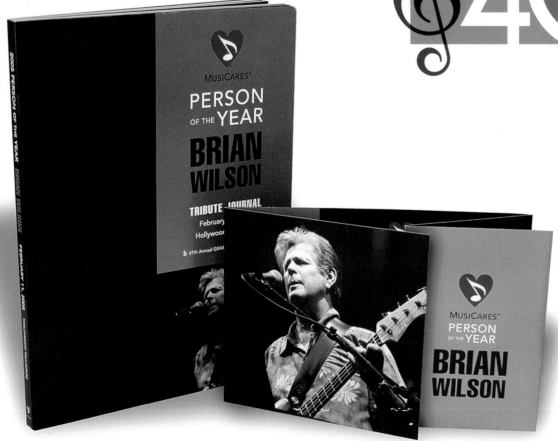

1 | 2 |

EVENT   The Recording Academy Honors

CLIENT   The Recording Academy

1

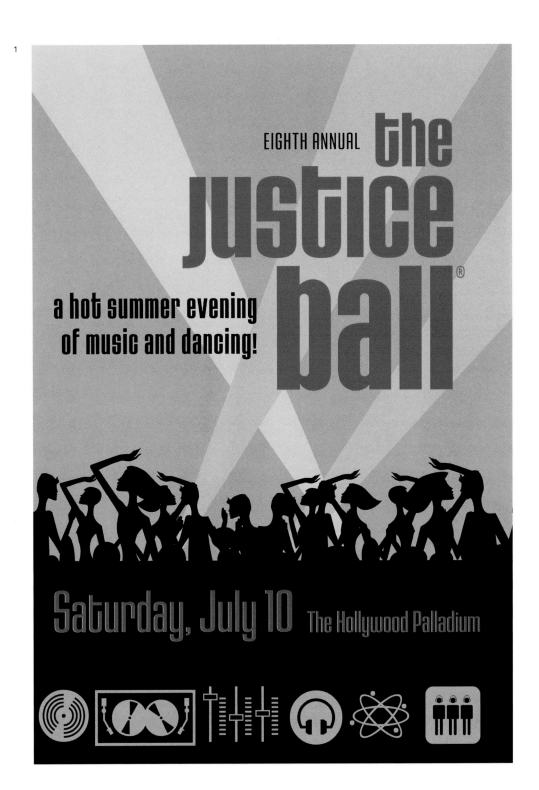

2

a FUTURE and a HOPE

General Conference of
Metropolitan Community Churches

July 21-26, 2005 • Calgary, Alberta, Canada

3

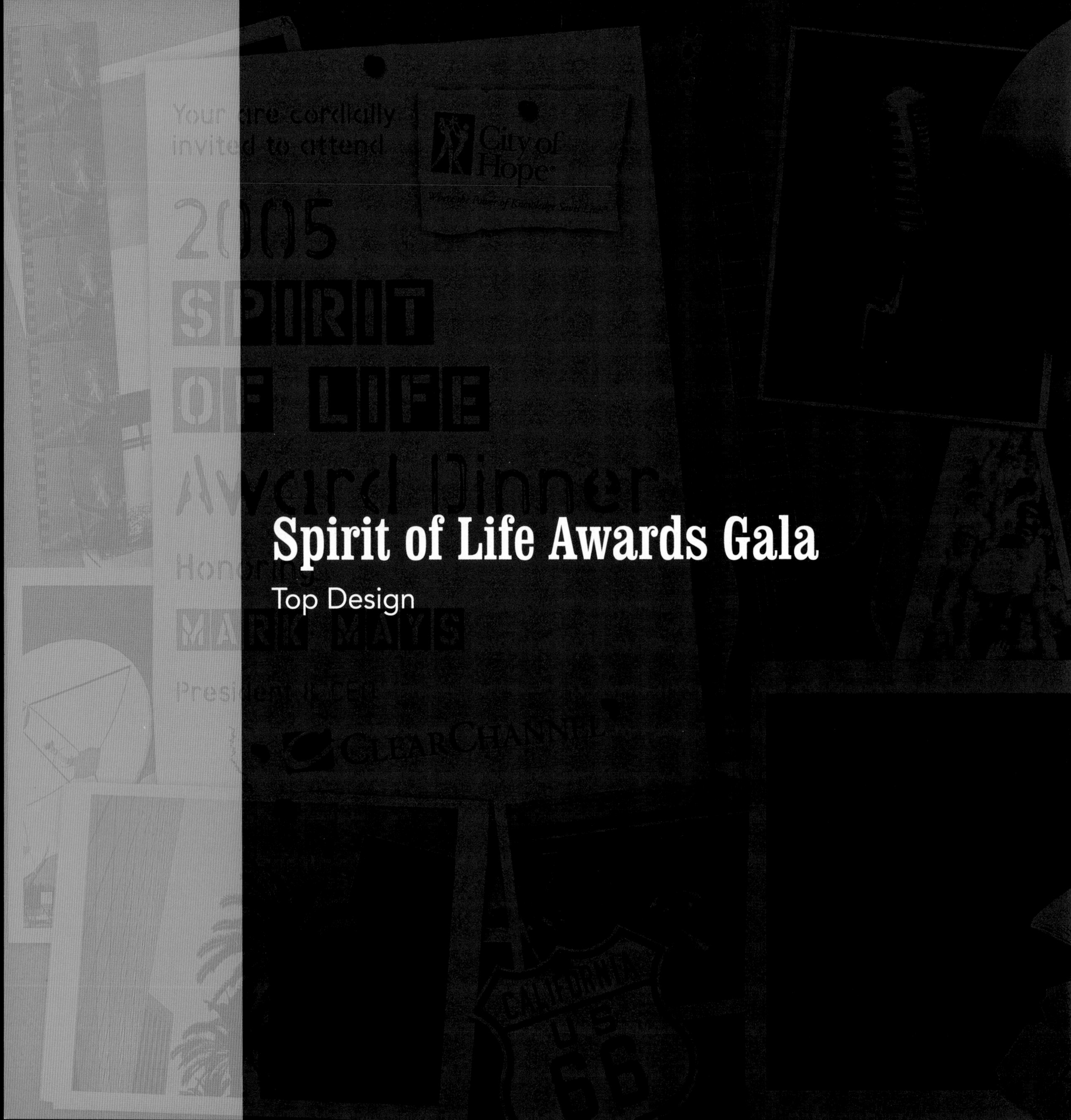

Spirit of Life Awards Gala

Top Design

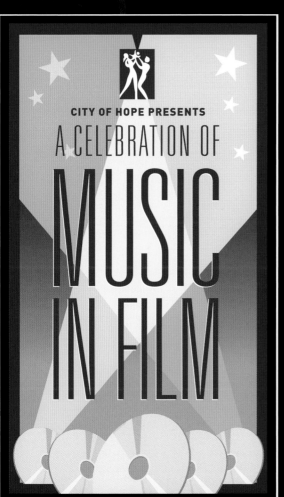

City of Hope is a leading research and treatment hospital specializing in the treatment of cancer, diabetes, and other life-threatening diseases.

It is known for its innovative fund-raising efforts and commitment to combating these serious ailments. As part of their philanthropic efforts, City of Hope has various industry-related committees that raise money and awareness. In Los Angeles, the Music and Entertainment Industry Committee holds an awards gala to present a Spirit of Life Award to an industry member who has made "a notable contribution to both their community and profession" and who have "fundamentally influenced the direction of the music industry." Each year, as many as 2,000 leaders in the music and entertainment fields attend this event, raising anywhere from $3 to $11 million dollars annually, making it one of Los Angeles' largest fund-raisers.

For the past thirteen years, Top Design has worked closely with City of Hope to create a look and feel for the fund-raising event. The biggest challenge has been reinventing the wheel each year, creating a completely new design, with the City of Hope logo as the only carried over element. Top Design creates a new event logo, invitation, and tribute journal

each year. The design process begins nearly five months prior to the event to allow time for research and production.

To set the design direction, the designers begin by learning as much as possible about that year's honoree. The design then stems from the honoree's personality, company, clients and the type of music they make. In 2002, each of the six honorees headed the music departments at major film studios, so the design incorporated the familiar iconography of a film reel on the invitation, journal book, and collateral. Similarly, when the head of *Billboard Magazine* was honored, the invitation resembled an issue of the magazine dubbed, "The Spirit of Life."

For the 2005 honoree, the CEO of Clear Channel Communications, one of the largest owner and operators of radio in the world, Top Design took a very modern and graphic approach by using a crowded bulletin board as its main inspiration with a laminated backstage pass as a complementary piece. The black and red color palette and the use of iconic imagery such as satellites, CDs, and a Route 66 sign played into the revived popularity of rock music at the time.

The Top Design team tries to utilize innovative printing techniques to ensure that the final piece is dynamic and elegant. For example, the

Your are cordially invited to attend

City of Hope®
Where the Power of Knowledge Saves Lives®

2005
SPIRIT
OF LIFE
Award Dinner

Honoring
MARK MAYS
President & CEO

ClearChannel

CALIFORNIA
US 66

OCTOBER 20, 2005
6:30pm Cocktail Reception
7:30pm Dinner & Program

Barker Hangar
Santa Monica

Attire: Black Tie
RSVP & Advertising
Information Enclosed

ADMIT ONE
ADMIT ONE

RSVP+ADVERTISING

City of Hope®

2005
SPIRIT
OF LIFE
Award Dinner

CITY OF HOPE

An innovative biomedical research, treatment
and educational institution, is dedicated
to the prevention and cure of cancer and
other life-threatening diseases, guided by a
compassionate, patient-centered philosophy
and supported by a national foundation of
humanitarian philanthropy.

a return to elegance

Please join us as City of Hope

Presents

"The Spirit of Life" Award

to

KENNETH "BABYFACE" EDMONDS

ANTONIO "L.A." REID

Wednesday Evening
October 29, 1997, 6:30 PM

at

Elegance Square, Century City

(Constellation between Century Park West & Avenue of the Stars)

For more information and reservations
call City of Hope at 213/892-7268

CITY OF HOPE touching the lives of millions

2006 piece had a simple black and silver color scheme, with refined lettering foil-stamped and embossed to embody the elegance and sophistication of the occasion.

Because Los Angeles is the epicenter of the entertainment industry and its associated events (i.e., film premieres, awards shows, etc), there is a very high standard for this type of high profile, music industry event. As such, the design for this event must have a distinctly LA look while still being interesting enough to stand out among the masses of other similar events. The trick is to avoid being cliché while still using imagery—like music notes or film reels—that is representative of the city and the entertainment industry. By using a music note with dimension and movement in 1997 and a film reel not just as imagery but as the whole invitation in 2002, Top Design captured the nostalgic familiarity associated with these icons but in a way that was fresh, interesting, and still relevant.

It is because Top Design is committed to creating pieces that are true to the honoree, City of Hope, and the Los Angeles music and film industry that they create such successful and memorable pieces for the Spirit of Life awards gala.

YOU ARE CORDIALLY INVITED TO JOIN US FOR THE

2006 SPIRIT OF LIFE AWARD DINNER

HONORING

CHARLES GOLDSTUCK

PRESIDENT AND COO
BERTELSMANN MUSIC GROUP U.S.

THURSDAY, OCTOBER 5, 2006

6:30PM COCKTAIL RECEPTION
7:30PM DINNER & PROGRAM

PACIFIC DESIGN CENTER
8687 MELROSE AVENUE, WEST HOLLYWOOD

BLACK TIE
RSVP AND ADVERTISING

★ EVENT COMMITTEES
★ MUSIC & ENTERTAINMENT INDUSTRY
EXECUTIVE COMMITTEE
★ ADVERTISING INFORMATION

City of Hope

TRIPLE PLATINUM
DOUBLE PLATINUM
PLATINUM

Tribute Journal Advertising

An innovative biomedical research, treatment and educational institution, is dedicated to the prevention and cure of cancer and other life-threatening diseases, guided by a compassionate, patient-centered philosophy and supported by a national foundation of humanitarian philanthropy.

★ 2006 **City of Hope** SPIRIT OF LIFE® AWARD
THURSDAY, OCTOBER 5, 2006

★ 2006 SPIRIT OF LIFE AWARD **City of Hope®**

ART & DESIGN

1 |

EVENT   28th Annual Art Deco Weekend
CLIENT   Miami Design Preservation League
DESIGN   Laura Smith Illustration

2 |

EVENT   Come Find Your Grit
CLIENT   AIGA/Austin
DESIGN   Laura Smith Illustration

1

2

1

2

1 |
EVENT   Painted Music
CLIENT   Katzen Museum
DESIGN   Chemi Montes Design

2 |
EVENT   Spectacular Vernacular Tour
CLIENT   Los Angeles Conservancy
DESIGN   Chris Green Design

1

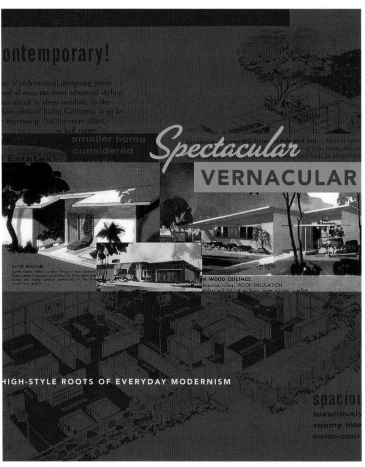

2

1 | 2 |

EVENT   Creative Best 2002

CLIENT   Columbus Society of
Communicating Arts

DESIGN   Element

1

2

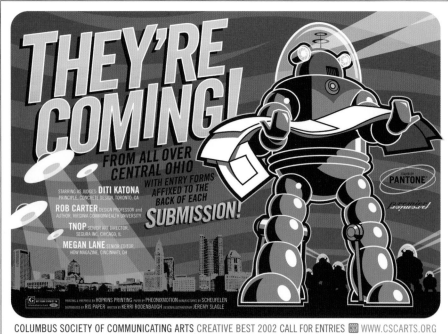

1 |

EVENT   Serious Moonlight

CLIENT Cranbrook Academy of Art
        and Art Museum

DESIGN Conversant Studios

2 |

EVENT   Better Than A Stick in the Eye

CLIENT AIGA Wichita

DESIGN Dotzero Design

1

2

1 |

EVENT   Art Seen through the Writers'
        Eyes: Readings of Poetry and
        Prose Inspired by Art

CLIENT Cranbrook Art Museum

DESIGN Conversant Studios

2 |

EVENT   Portfolio Showcase

CLIENT The Freelance Exchange
        of Kansas City

DESIGN Reactor

3 |

EVENT   AIGA LA Patron's Night 2006

CLIENT Emma, Inc.

DESIGN Emma, Inc.

1

2

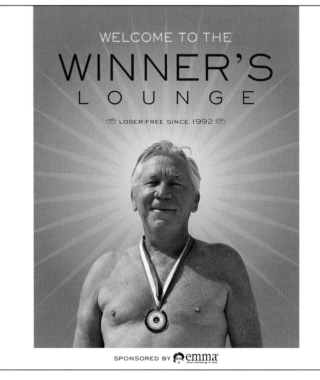

3

1 |
EVENT   Departure Lounge National
         Architecture Conference,
         Melbourne
CLIENT   RAIA
DESIGN   Fabio Ongarato Design

2 |
EVENT   Nordex
CLIENT   Seattle Design Center,
         Davis Agency
DESIGN   Dotzero Design

1

2

1 | 2 |

EVENT   AIGA Indianapolis Power Lunch,
         with Joe Duffy

CLIENT   AIGA Indy

DESIGN   Funnel

1

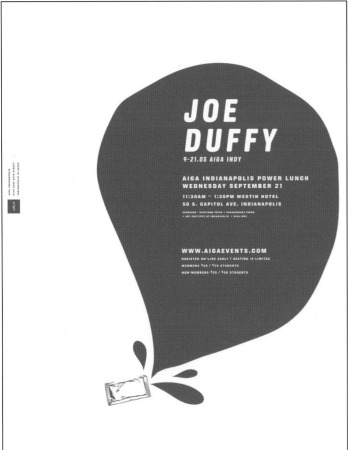

2

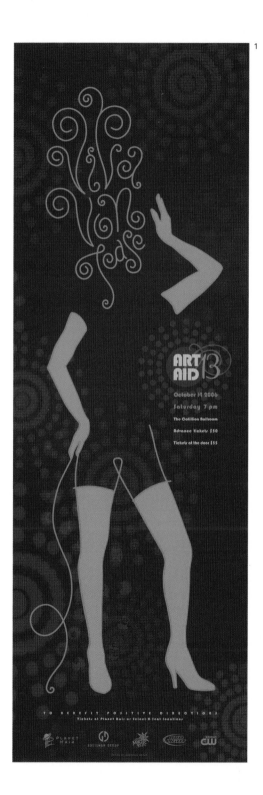

1

P E N R O D
ARTS FAIR

2

1 |
EVENT   Art Aid 13 Viva Von Tease
CLIENT   Positive Directions
DESIGN   Greteman Group

2 | 3 |
EVENT   Penrod Arts Fair
CLIENT   Penrod Society
DESIGN   Funnel

3

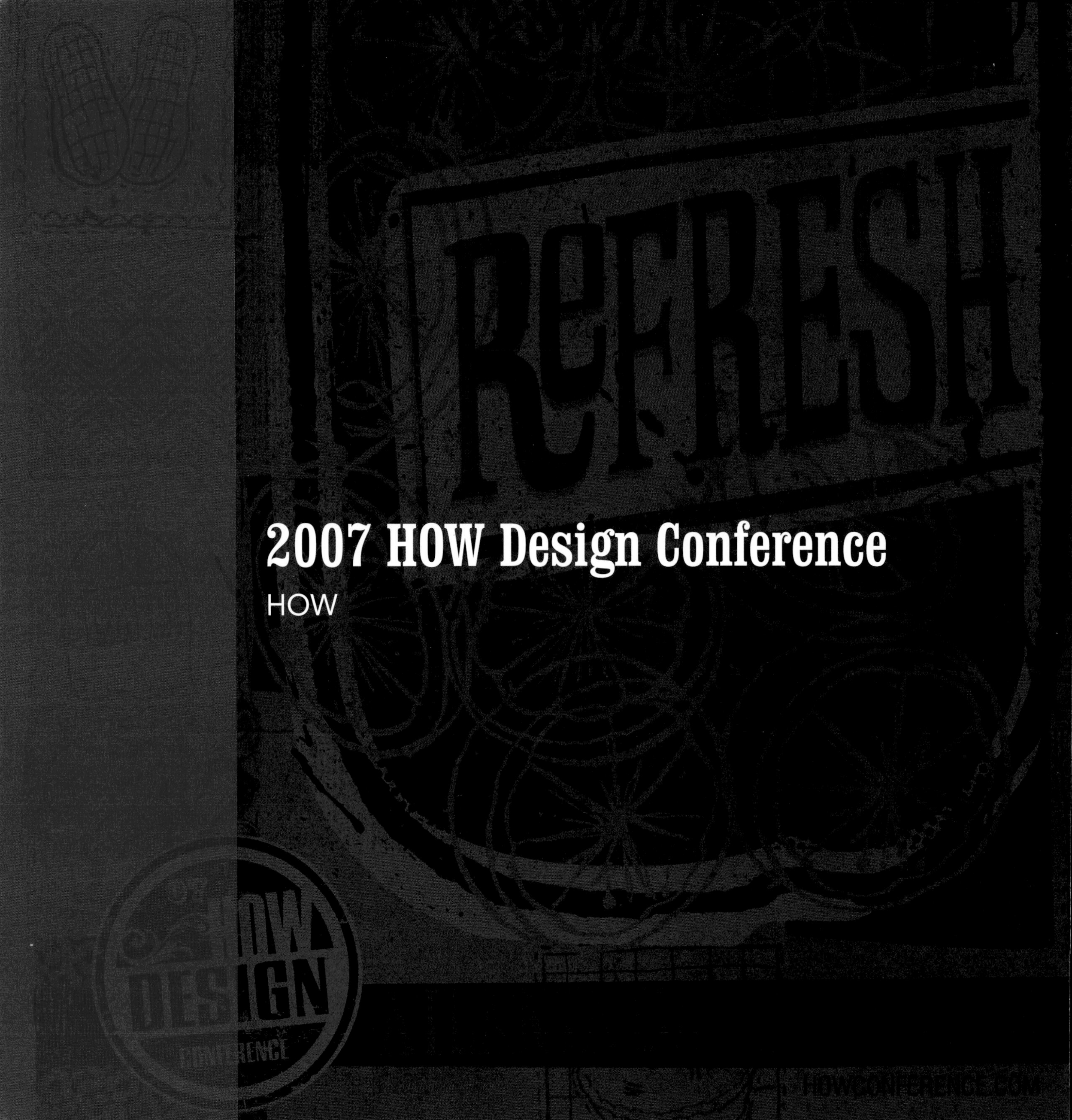

2007 HOW Design Conference

HOW

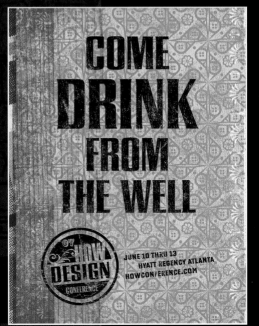

JUNE 10 THRU 13
HYATT REGENCY ATLANTA
HOWCONFERENCE.COM

Each year, F&W Publications, parent company of HOW Magazine, puts together the HOW Design Conference (HDC) for creative professionals from around the world.

The goal of this event is to provide graphic designers, art directors, illustrators, principals, and students with an opportunity to be "exposed to timely, real world, practical information, and new strategies, and techniques relevant to the graphic design industry." The conference offers attendees many opportunities, including attending presentations and workshops conducted by graphic design leaders. There's also a resource center where companies, such as paper and software manufacturers, display and promote new products and techniques. But perhaps the most important aspect of the HDC is the opportunity to network with other creative professionals and leaders in the field. This event attracts nearly 4,000 creative professionals each year and is the most widely attended conference of its kind in the United States. It provides an enlightening and comfortable environment wherein attendees and featured speakers can commingle in a relaxed, friendly environment and is also widely attended by sponsors and exhibitors who recognize the opportunity to market to and interact directly with their target audience.

LIMITED-EDITION 2007
HOW DESIGN CONFERENCE POSTER

For the 2007 HDC, the Creative Services team from F&W Publications and a contract writer worked together to create concepts for the conference's design direction. They were ultimately responsible for the entire campaign of materials, from project management and conceptualization, through design and execution. The components of this campaign included: the event logo, ads and teasers for publication in HOW and Print magazines, posters, stationery, binders, brochures, postcards, a website, T-shirts, and signage. The creative team began their work ten months prior to the event date, with a timeline of two weeks to six months for designing each element, but many of the teasers and advertisements had to be produced within the first few months. Although there were a great many pieces to be designed, they were approached piece by piece with realistic goals and deadlines.

The conference's design concept blended imagery, color, typography, and copy to create a familiar, friendly and welcoming personality relevant to the location and content. The collateral materials were designed to be "clever, thoughtful, aesthetically appealing, and verbally engaging." Knowing that the key to charming designers was "all in the details," the design approach had to be thorough and cohesive.

While in Atlanta, Georgia, for a preconference on-site visit, the designers photographed local design and culture, from wallpaper patterns found in boutiques and restaurants, to flyers found on

[9] ASK QUESTIONS.

This year's conference lineup boasts a record 54 **speakers** from design studios, corporate creative departments and consultancies throughout the U.S. and Canada. A veritable gaggle of creative minds—all in one place, ready to field your questions about design, technology and the creative business. So start your list now, bring it with you to Atlanta and fire away. We don't call it the HOW Conference for nothin'.

1. **Shelley Armstrong** Microsoft/Xbox 2. **David C. Baker** ReCourse, Inc. 3. **Gary Baseman** Baseman Studios 4. **Matteo Bologna** Mucca Design 5. **Russell Brown** Adobe Systems, Inc. 6. **Roy Burns** Stoltze Design 7. **Kathy Barton** The Creative Group 8. **Sheila Campbell** Wild Blue Yonder, Inc. 9. **Jeff Carlson** Never Enough Coffee Creations 10. **Joshua C. Chen** Chen Design Associates 11. **Sharon Clark** Sayles Graphic Design 12. **Bob Connolly** onRevolve 13. **Jim Coudal** Coudal Partners 14. **Hillman Curtis** hillmancurtis, inc. 15. **Chuck Dieseel** The Chank Company 16. **Dave Drimalas** Hybrid Design 17. **Terri Edelman** The Edelman Group 18. **Brian Edelson** Whirlpool Corporation 19. **Leatrice Eiseman** Eiseman Center for Color Information and Training 20. **Chris Elkerton** Shaga Creative 21. **Marc English** Marc English Design 22. **Brian Flynn** Hybrid Design 23. **Steff Grimshalter** CMG Partners 24. **Steve Gordon Jr.** RDQLUS Design Quarters 25. **Dave Gouveia** 3 Dogz Creative 26. **Denny Gregory** McHenryBrown 27. **Florence Maridon** Gathering

18 | 19

28. **Sam Harrison** Ideas•Words•Actions 29. **Jeni Herberger** DesignMatters 30. **Cyrus Highsmith** Font Bureau 31. **Kit Hinrichs** Pentagram 32. **Chip Kidd** Alfred A. Knopf 33. **Jim Krause** Jim Krause Design 34. **Wili Lidwell** Stuff Creative Design Studio 35. **Kevin McConkey** gripdesign 36. **Claudia McCue** Practicalia, LLC 37. **Pamela Mitchell** The Reinvention Institute, Inc. 38. **Jay Reiten** Design Tools Monthly 40. **Michael Nissens** lynda.com 40. **Chip Pearson** JAMF Software 41. **Jean Parvin** The Law Offices of Jean S. Perwin 42. **Jodie Peters** Northwestern Mutual 43. **Hank Richardson** Portfolio Center 44. **Matthew Richmond** The Chopping Block 45. **Clifford Risoto** Risoto Design 46. **Deborah Rossman** Summera/Pegus & Company 47. **Daniel Schutzsmith** Graphic Define 48. **Roberto de Vivo de Cumptich** devio & co. 51. **Armin Vit** Pentagram 52. **Scott Wadler** MTV Networks 53. **Dave Werner** River Studios, Okay Samurai Multimedia 54. **Sharon Werner** Werner Design Werks, Inc.

20 | 21

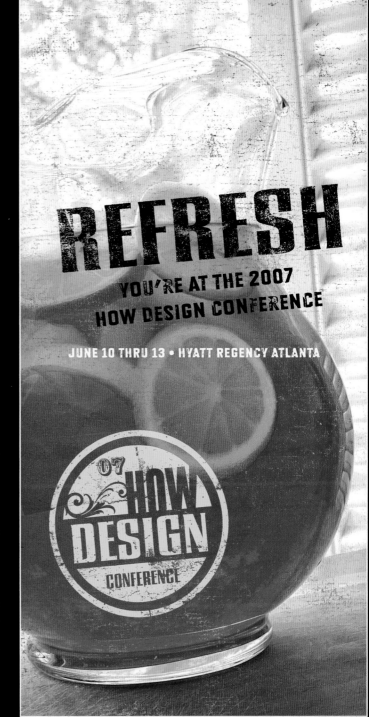

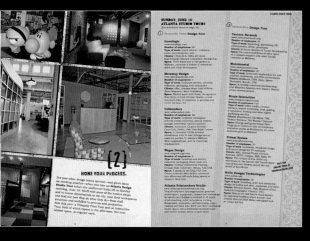

telephone polls, and billboards. They compiled a library of all things related to Atlanta that included visuals, words, and phrases. The design was a natural progression of the many things they encountered there, much of which had a handcrafted look they endeavored to capture. This also led to the development of a woodblock typographic approach that created cohesiveness between the imagery and typography.

Once the direction was established, the creative team developed a visual personality they could mix and match among the different pieces to create an array of fresh and interesting pieces. They developed a circular, stamplike logo that would be used on all of the final pieces that added to the overall handcrafted feel of the materials. The warm color palette, with backgrounds and textures resembling tablecloths, school paper, and a quilt, created a visual landscape that was as familiar and welcoming as it was interesting and attractive. Incorporating ornamental elements and weathering effects gave further impact to these elements. The marriage of visual texture with key words such as "refresh," "refuel," "sweet," and "peachy" conveyed to prospective attendees that this Atlanta-based event would reenergize their creativity.

The 2007 HOW Design Conference owes a great deal of its success to the creative team in charge of defining and designing its personality. Though challenged by just how to accomplish this task and how to use copy in a way that would appeal to people in all stages of their design careers, the creative team was skillfully able to build a collage of imagery and words that, when applied to event materials, created not just attractive packaging but also gave a window into the special product housed within.

WELCOME TO HOW.

The HOW Design Conference isn't just sessions–it's about making new connections. And that's as easy said as done, whether you attend the networking kickoff or just chat up your fellow attendees between sessions. So get out there and strike up a conversation with a stranger. You never know what you might learn.

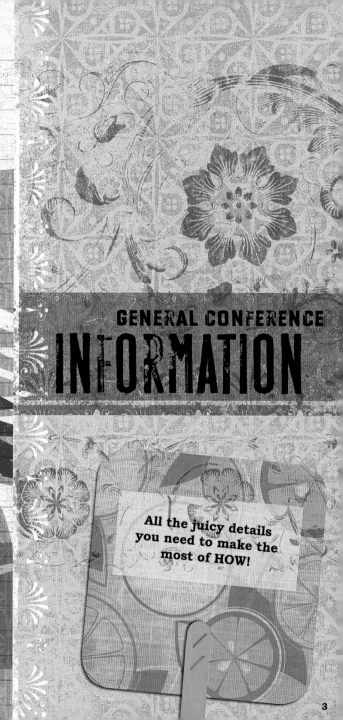

GENERAL CONFERENCE
INFORMATION

All the juicy details you need to make the most of HOW!

1 |

EVENT   Philadelphia University
            Spring Lecture Series

CLIENT   Philadelphia University

DESIGN   Kradel Design

2 |

EVENT   Feedback 8

CLIENT   AIGA Philadelphia

DESIGN   Kradel Design

3 |

EVENT   Art in the Park

CLIENT   Kutztown Community
            Partnership

DESIGN   Kradel Design

4 |

EVENT   The Heads of State Lecture

CLIENT   Philadelphia University

DESIGN   Kradel Design

1

2

3
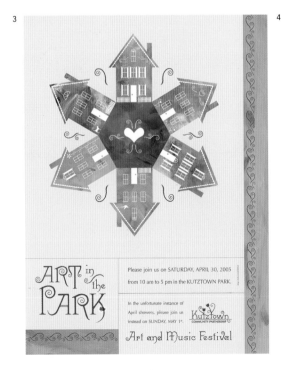

4
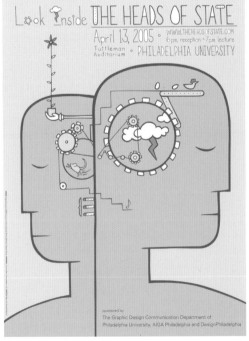

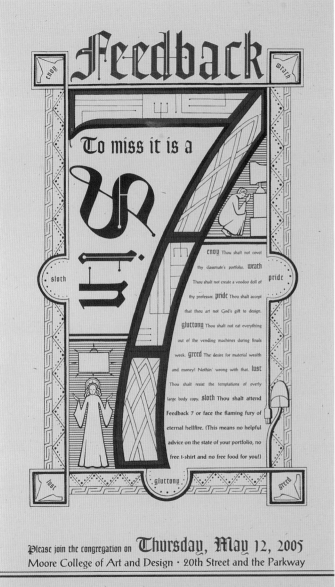

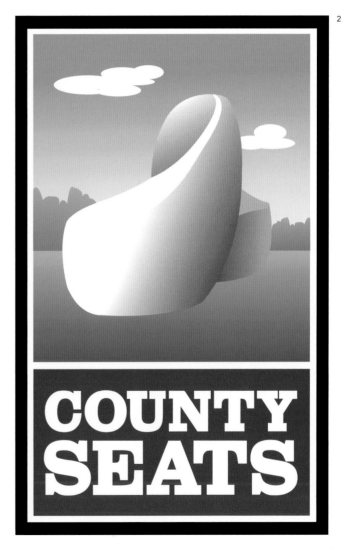

1 |
EVENT   7 Exhibitions of Modest Size
CLIENT   Chop Suey Books Gallery
DESIGN   Kate Resnick

1

1 |
EVENT   Paul Sahre Lecture
CLIENT   Philadelphia University
DESIGN   Kradel Design

1

1 |

EVENT   Revolutions
CLIENT   Forest Lawn Museum
DESIGN   Michael Doret/Alphabet Soup

2 |

EVENT   Sayles Graphic Design/Des Moines
          Playhouse Poster Exhibit 2007
CLIENT   Sayles Graphic Design
DESIGN   Sayles Graphic Design

3 |

EVENT   Mix 'N' Match
CLIENT   Northwest Arkansas Art
          Director's Club
DESIGN   Michael Doret/Alphabet Soup

4 |

EVENT   Coast to Coast
CLIENT   Art Director's Association of Iowa
DESIGN   Michael Doret/Alphabet Soup

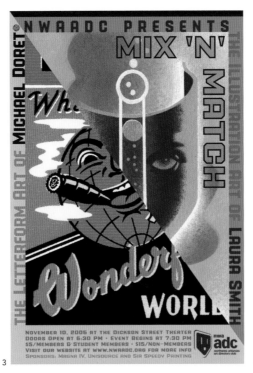

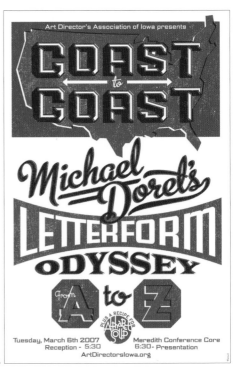

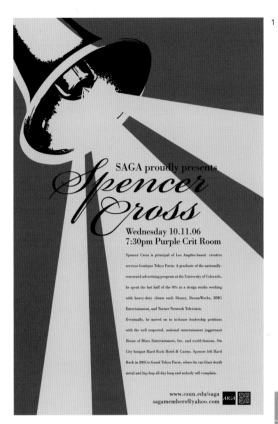

1 |

EVENT   Spencer Cross Speaker Event

CLIENT   Student Advertising Graphics
Association (SAGA)

DESIGN   SAGA

2 | 3 |

EVENT   Guild Lounge

CLIENT   Graphic Arts Guild LA

DESIGN   RED Studios

2

guild lounge

3

1 |
EVENT   Creative Bloc 7
CLIENT   Cedar Rapids Ad Federation
DESIGN   Sayles Graphic Design

2 |
EVENT   + E Awards
CLIENT   New Mexico Advertising Awards
DESIGN   Rome & Gold Creative

1

2

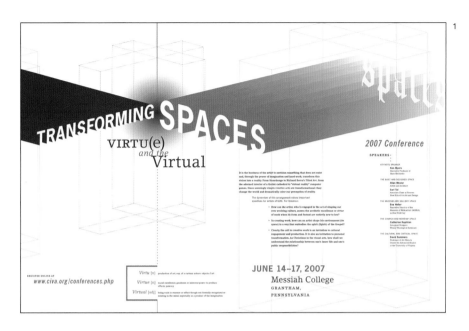

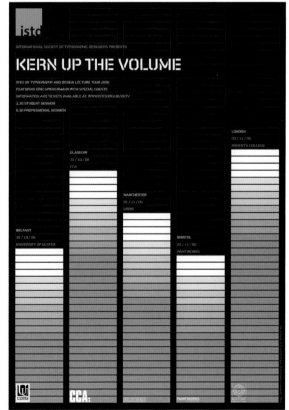

1

2

1 |

EVENT   12 Japanese Masters
CLIENT   Tyler School of Art
DESIGN   Scorsone/Drueding

2 |

EVENT   Design Army Presentation
CLIENT   Tyler School of Art
DESIGN   Scorsone/Drueding

3 |

EVENT   Baltimore Artscape
CLIENT   Artscape
DESIGN   substance151

3

1

2

3

1 | 2 | 3 |

EVENT   TypeCon 2006

CLIENT   Society of Typographic
          Aficionados

DESIGN   Stoltze Design

1

2

3

1 | 2 | 3 | 4 | 5 | 6 | 7 |

EVENT   Design Forum Sochi 2005
CLIENT   Union of Designers of Russia
DESIGN   Stavitsky Design

4

5

6

7

1

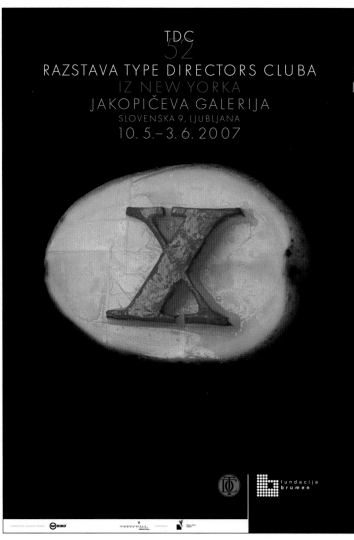

2

1 | 2 |

EVENT   TDC52, Type Directors Club
          Exhibition in Slovenia

CLIENT   Fundacija Brumen

DESIGN   Tomato Kosir, s.p.

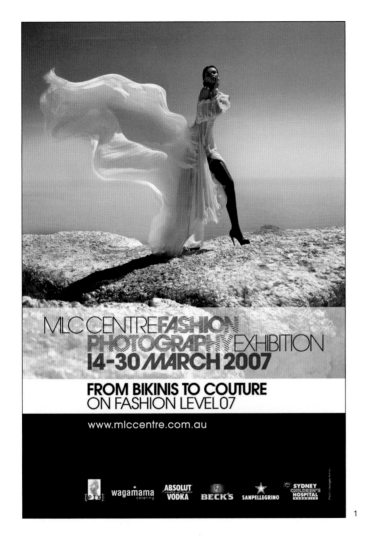

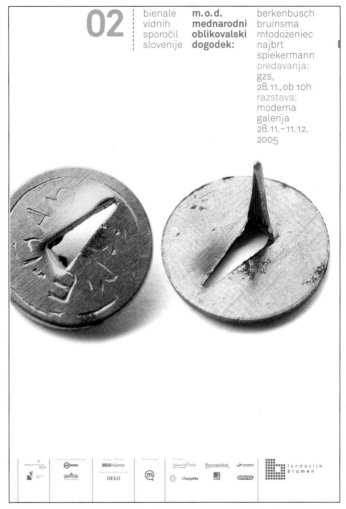

02

bienale   m.o.d.   berkenbusch
vidnih   mednarodni   bruinsma
sporočil   oblikovalski   młodożeniec
slovenije   dogodek: najbrt
                                   spiekermann
                                   predavanja:
                                   gzs,
                                   28.11., ob 10h
                                   razstava:
                                   moderna
                                   galerija
                                   28.11.–11.12.
                                   2005

1 |

EVENT   Destination Fashion

CLIENT   MLC Centre

DESIGN   THERE

2 |

EVENT   M.O.D. International Design Event

CLIENT   Fundacija Brumen

DESIGN   Tomato Kosir s.p.

3 |

EVENT   SEEing Green

CLIENT   AIGA LA

DESIGN   UNIT design Collective

Thinking Creatively Conference

The Design Studio at Kean University

an event geared toward graphic designers with the purpose of encouraging innovation, experimentation, and creative thinking in the working environment, and in life. Steven Brower, art director of the Design Studio at Kean University, identified his goal as being, "to educate and elevate. And to have a good time." Being the only event of this nature in New Jersey, the audience of creative professionals, educators, and students, always finds it an enlightening experience to interact with leading speakers from the design industry.

Brower and his team design and oversee all materials for the conference. These materials include: invitations, posters, postcards, event booklets, bags, pens, T-shirts, event signage, advertisements, and Web, and on-screen graphics. To promote the event, posters, postcards, and programs are sent to various schools, institutions, corporations, design firms, and individual attendees. The posters, pins, pens, and bags are giveaways at the event.

In 2004, the first year of the conference, Brower designed a poster for his keynote speech that was inspired by a Dadaist game he played as a child with his father and sister. In this game, several people contribute to a drawing or sentence without any knowledge of what the previous contributor has done. The name of this creative exercise, The Exquisite Corpse, is derived from the first sentence that was created in this

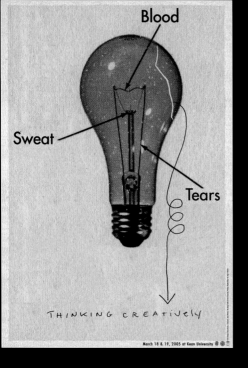

way: "The-exquisite-corpse-will-drink-new-wine." For the poster, Brower collaborated with Milton Glaser, Mirko Ilic, and Luba Lukova, each of whom contributed one panel of the drawing. The resulting image—Groucho Marx with angel wings on a farm and drawing in his own right foot—perfectly captures the spirit of this conference. The idea is to think in a completely new way, to create as though there is no beginning or end. As a design for the inaugural conference, Brower sent a clear message that this was an event unlike any other.

In each of the following four years, Brower followed up his Exquisite Corpse poster with equally interesting and thought-provoking designs. In 2005, he used a lightbulb, a symbol for revelation, to illustrate the idea that blood, sweat, tears, and creative thinking are all necessary parts for uncovering a great idea. The following year, he used a simple illustration of a pen and a multicolored octopus to illustrate the simplicity of thinking differently.

In 2007, inspired by popular packaging, he took a typographic approach, combining some letters and using others in different directions, in eye-catching colors and a design so complex you need to see it more than once to catch the subtlety of its cleverness. Through the first four years of the conference, Brower came up with entirely new ideas, but for the upcoming fifth year, he intends to incorporate some of this earlier work into the design.

Each year, Steven Brower designed an entirely new look and feel for the Thinking Creatively Conference, attempting to create something unexpected, interesting, and out-of-the-ordinary. He designed pieces

that embody the core philosophy of the conference itself. They are so unusual that he claims that these designs are usually met with either an "ah!" or a "huh?" This conference is about cultivating experimentation, risk taking, and inventiveness amongst creatives. Though he may leave a few confused, Brower consistently produces pieces that are fresh, interesting, and truly embody the message of the Thinking Creatively Conference.

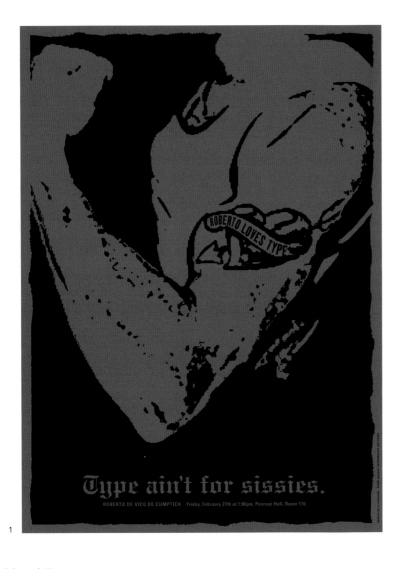

1 |
EVENT   Roberto de Vicq
         de Cumptich Lecture

CLIENT   Tyler School of Art

DESIGN   Tyler School of Art

2 |
EVENT   Sergio Leone Exhibit

CLIENT   Autry National Center

DESIGN   DISTINC

3 |
EVENT   F*in Design

CLIENT   AIGA San Francisco

DESIGN   MINE™

1 "Bison for Blankets"

"Hides for Horses"

You are cordially invited to trade this card for festivities at the Members' Exhibition Special Preview of

Encounters: The Fur Trade
Saturday, June 11, 2005, 10 am–5 pm
Autry National Center, Griffith Park

Join us as we explore the fascinating story of the fur trade and how it linked individuals, families, and communities while creating blended cultures in the early 19th-century American West.

Open to all Autry National Center members.
This invitation is nontransferable. Please show your membership card for admittance.

This members-only event features:

· Preview of *Encounters: The Fur Trade*, featuring 4 handsewn trading post pelts
· Members-only specials in the café and Museum Store
· Presentation by curator Dr. Louise Pubols
· Live music from the Multicultural Music and Art Foundation of Northridge
· *Traders and trappers'* encampment featuring costumed reenactors
· Lakota storytelling performance by the Bordeaux-Vigil family
· Two panel discussions: *Animals: Food, Fashion, or Family?* and *What's West, What's Next: The Future of the Western Past*

Autry National Center

4700 Western Heritage Way · Los Angeles, CA 90027 · 323.667.2000 · autrynationalcenter.org

2

The Fur Trade
LIMITED TIME ONLY AT THE AUTRY · GRIFFITH PARK

Autry National Center

1 | 2 |
EVENT   Encounters: The Fur Trade
CLIENT   Autry National Center
DESIGN   DISTINC

1

Program: ISEA2006   San José, California, United States   International Symposium on Electronic Art

2

ex XX :: post position
20 years of mfa graduates from CADRE
laboratory for new media @ san josé state university
CADRE = computers in art, design, research, and education

exhibition on view ::
7/18/06 through 8/13/06

performances ::
tuesday, august 8, 7pm
with zeroone opening night gallery crawl. free!

3

 | 2 | 3 |

EVENT   ISEA 2006 (International
         Symposium on Electronic Art)

CLIENT   ZeroOne/ISEA

DESIGN   Joe Miller's Company

1

1 | 2 | 3 |
EVENT   Artist's Ball Six: Stanlee's Brain
CLIENT   Yerba Buena Center for the Arts
DESIGN   Elixir Design

2

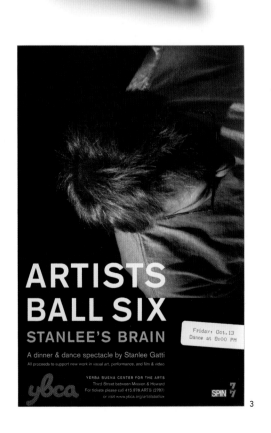

3

1 |
EVENT   Bellevue Sculpture Exhibition
CLIENT City of Bellevue
DESIGN Kendall Ross

2 |
EVENT   AIGA Design Conference
CLIENT AIGA Boston
DESIGN Stoltze Design

1

2

1

2

1 |
EVENT   Star Wars Costume Exhibition
CLIENT   The FIDM Museum
DESIGN   FIDM Publications

2 |
EVENT   Under the Big Top Art Show
CLIENT   ColorGraphics
DESIGN   Belyea

1

1 |

EVENT   Ruddygore

CLIENT   Belyea

DESIGN   Belyea

2 |

EVENT   Creative Best

CLIENT   Columbus Society of
          Communicating Arts

DESIGN   Element

2

1

1 | 2 |
EVENT   Von Dutch Exhibition
CLIENT   California State University
         Northridge (CSUN)
DESIGN   Tornado Design

2

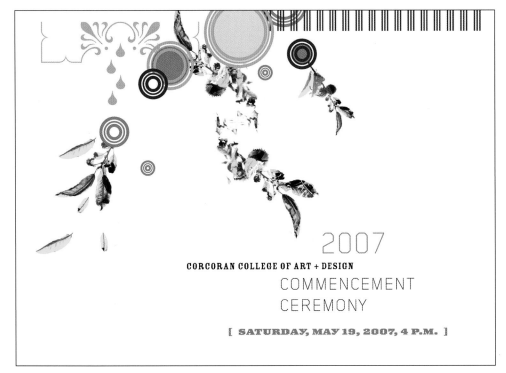

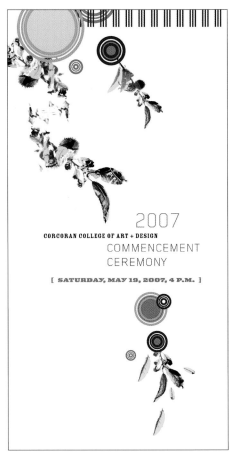

1

2

3

1 | 2 | 3 | 4 | 5 | 6 |

EVENT   2007 Corcoran Collage of
Art & Design's Senior Thesis
Exhibitions and Graduation
Commencement Ceremony

CLIENT   2007 Corcoran Collage of Art
& Design, Washington, DC

DESIGN   Conversant Studios

BUSINESS

1 |

EVENT   Reservoir Capital Holiday Party
CLIENT   Reservoir Capital
DESIGN   Synergy Graphix

1

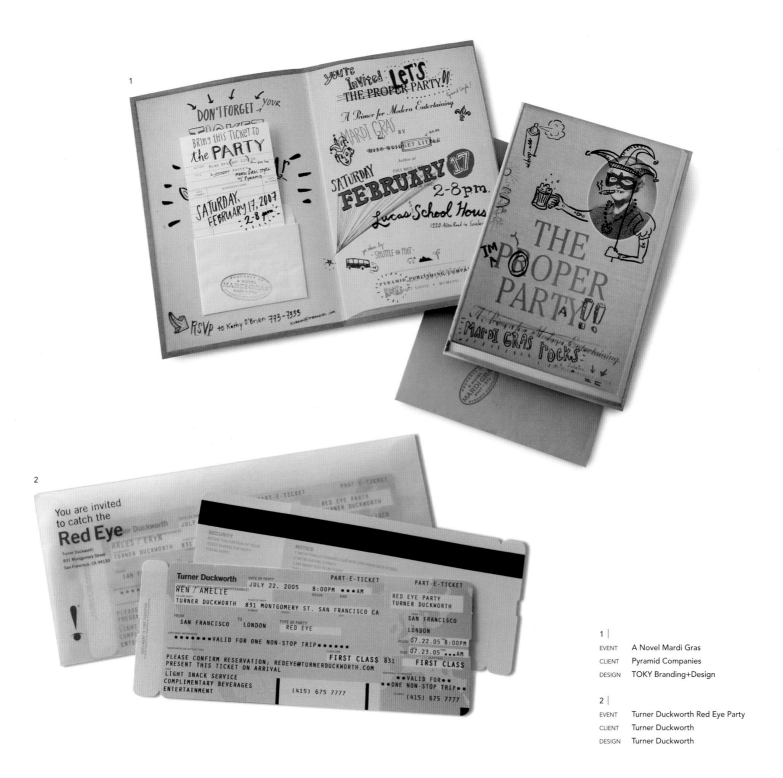

1 |
EVENT   A Novel Mardi Gras
CLIENT   Pyramid Companies
DESIGN   TOKY Branding+Design

2 |
EVENT   Turner Duckworth Red Eye Party
CLIENT   Turner Duckworth
DESIGN   Turner Duckworth

1 |
EVENT   Building Women Annual Luncheon
CLIENT   Countrywide Home Loans
          Mercer Island
DESIGN   View Design Company

2 |
EVENT   Kaikoura Seafest
CLIENT   Kaikoura Promotions
DESIGN   Lloyds Graphic Design Ltd

1

You are Cordially Invited to…

BUILDING
Women
ANNUAL LUNCHEON 2007

Honoring Inspiring Women
in the Building Industry

MAY 10 • THE EDGEWATER HOTEL

Please join us as we pay tribute to five extraordinary women whose pioneering contributions to the building industry have inspired us.

Enjoy a festive luncheon and learn more about the new **Women in Building Mentorship Program**, sponsored by the Master Builders Education Foundation. Proceeds from the luncheon will seed this exciting new program.

Thursday, May 10, 2007
11:30 am —1:00 pm
• Awards Presentation
• Speaker: Amanda Murphy, Working With Power, LLC
• Lunch

The Edgewater Hotel
2411 Alaskan Way, Pier 67
Seattle, WA 98121

Admission: $60
Includes $20 donation to the Master Builders Education Foundation

REGISTER OR DONATE ONLINE:
Go to www.fernacity.com and click on "Useful Links" in the top menu.

FOR MORE INFORMATION:
Christine Kenyon, 206.275.5709

2007 HONOREES
Contributions to Industry
CATHY GASPAR
Co-owner, Gaspars Construction Inc.

Contributions to Community
ADA HEALEY
Vice President of Real Estate, Vulcan, Inc.

Philanthropy
JULIA CORDERO
Student, SCCC Wood Construction Program

Education
RENA M. KLEIN, FAIA
Principal, RM Klein Consulting

Sales & Marketing
LESLIE WILLIAMS
President, Williams Marketing

2

1

EVENT   C3 Speakeasy

CLIENT   C3 Vendors and Clients

DESIGN   C3 — Creative Consumer
Concepts

1 |
EVENT   C3 Honky Tonk Holiday
CLIENT   C3 Vendors and Clients
DESIGN   CC3 — Creative Consumer
          Concepts

2 |
EVENT   C3 Holiday Party
CLIENT   C3 Vendors and Clients
DESIGN   C3 — Creative Consumer
          Concepts

3 |
EVENT   C3 Holiday Royale
CLIENT   C3 Vendors and Clients
DESIGN   C3 — Creative Consumer
          Concepts

3

1

EVENT   Wallace Church Tuna Party 2006
CLIENT   Wallace Church, Inc.
DESIGN   Wallace Church, Inc.

2 | 3

EVENT   Wallace Church Tuna Party 2005
CLIENT   Wallace Church, Inc.
DESIGN   Wallace Church, Inc.

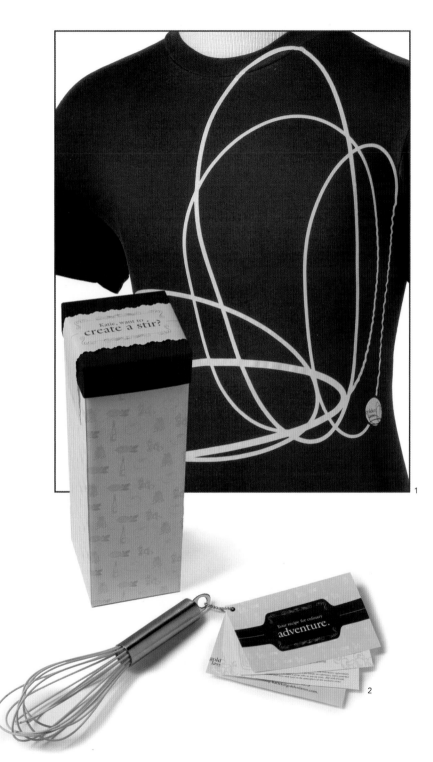

1 |
EVENT   Wallace Church Baseball
CLIENT   Wallace Church, Inc.
DESIGN   Wallace Church, Inc.

1

1 |
EVENT   Sycamore Hockey
CLIENT   Sycamore Networks
DESIGN   Silverscape, LLC.

2 |
EVENT   GES Grand Slam Gala
CLIENT   GES
DESIGN   CDI Studios

1 |
EVENT   Lawson Luncheon
CLIENT   Historic Lawson
DESIGN   Eye Design Studio

2 |
EVENT   Deep in the Heart of Texas
CLIENT   AtheroGenics, Inc.
DESIGN   The Jones Group

1 |
EVENT   Holiday Party 2006
CLIENT   Tom Fowler, Inc.
DESIGN   Tom Fowler, Inc.

2 |
EVENT   Holiday Party Luncheon 2006
CLIENT   Tom Fowler, Inc.
DESIGN   Tom Fowler, Inc.

Doll Capital Management Holiday Parties

Gee + Chung Design

Bogo Asian Fusion

EVENT ARTISTS

Asian Art Museum
200 Larkin Street
San Francisco
CA 94102

Valet Services
Provided

Holiday Attire

Doll Capital Management (DCM) is a venture capital firm with offices in San Francisco, California, and Beijing, China.

They focus their efforts on new and emerging technologies, believing that soon "every person in the world will be connected via the Internet: wired or wireless, desktop or wearable, visually or audibly, night and day." To this end, DCM invests in entrepreneurs with technological products that will move us closer to this eventuality. Each year, DCM throws a themed holiday party to reach out to its partners and clients.

DCM's party motifs are carried through the design and event atmosphere thoroughly and with purpose. Gee + Chung Design of San Francisco built a comprehensive graphics system for each event. The themes for these parties are represented on everything from the event invitations (both in print and online), to event banners, and both decorative and way-finding signage. While the themes are diverse, each one had a common message: internationalism. DCM wanted to communicate to their clients and partners that they have international expertise, global resources, and maintains close ties to the Chinese technological marketplace.

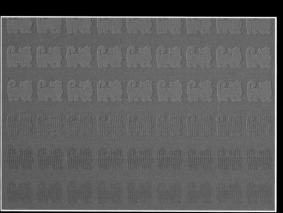

This global message is obvious in the design for the invitation for the "Spirit of the Holidays" party held at the Asian Art Museum of San Francisco, a double-sided mask with Santa Claus on one side and a Chinese spirit on the other. The piece demonstrates that there are two faces to this one company and reminds their clients of the close ties to the Asian market.

The 2006 "Year of the Dog" party in honor of the Chinese New Year also accomplished this with an eye-catching invitation in a striking color palette of red and gold on a pop-up of a beautiful gold dog.

The "Passport to the Holidays" party was closely related to the internationalism theme. It featured a vinyl paper invitation that very convincingly mimicked an actual passport, including stamps representing food from around the world, lists of international currencies and climates, and most importantly, a map of DCM's international portfolio companies.

The purpose of these parties is to allow their business partners to interact with the staff and to further establish the importance and prominence of DCM to its clients and entrepreneurs. As such, the design of these events not only had to represent the theme of the party, but also had to incorporate the DCM identity in an appropriate and tasteful way. Gee + Chung incorporated the DCM letters wherever possible, sometimes as simply as using them as graphic elements within an invitation or by using them to add to the texture of a design.

As seen in the "Spirit of the Holidays" invitation, the letters are presented in a slightly different color in various places on the invitation creating a depth beyond the simple two-dimensional format. The passport invitation featured the DCM letters on each page as either a background or decorative element. The "Year of the Dog" invitation and event logo incorporated the DCM letters in the dog symbol that served as the main decorative element. The clever design has both round and straight elements that can be purposed to mimic the shape

Security Check Point

Registration Desk

Approaching Entertainment Zone

Dance Heads straight ahead

Baggage Claim

Check your coat and any other carry-on items during your journey.

1st Floor, South Side

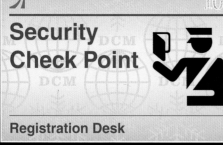

Passport Photos

Choose Beijing, Tokyo or Bombay as your destination.
Photography by Jan Lundberg

1st Floor, North Side

Museum Tours

Explore the scenic culture of the Far East. Docent-led tours available until 9:00pm.

2nd Floor, outside Samsung Hall

or appearance of teeth, a collar, or the toes, and nails of the dog's paw. Each invitation incorporated the letters and branding in a way that was at once subtle and apparent to create a visual texture.

Each year, DCM hopes to provide a holiday party and networking opportunity for its clients that would also convey the company's role as a leading international venture capital firm. In choosing to strategically theme and design these parties, they are making sure that these goals are not overlooked nor confused. The Gee + Chung Design team consistently came up with original, elegant, and interesting designs that were sure to capture the viewers attention and present their client as a leader in international venture capitalism.

1 |
EVENT   Real Art 20th Anniversary
CLIENT   Real Art Design Group, Inc.
DESIGN   Real Art Design Group, Inc.

2 |
EVENT   EarthShift Expo
CLIENT   EarthShift
DESIGN   Campbell Fisher Design

1

2

EARTHSHIF⌐

1 | 2 |
EVENT   Rock 'n Roll Wine AMP'd Festival
CLIENT   Rock 'n Roll Wine
DESIGN   CDI Studios

3 |
EVENT   Music to Your Ears
CLIENT   South African Post Office
DESIGN   Red Rocket Design & Advertising

1 | 2 | 3 | 4 |
EVENT   Imbizo—The Call of Africa
CLIENT   South African Post Office
DESIGN   Red Rocket Design & Advertising

2

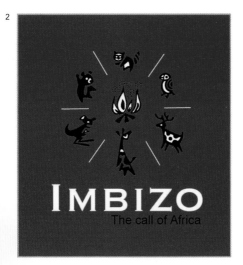

1

EVENT   French Bistro 75

CLIENT   Culinary Adventures

DESIGN   Kira Evans Design

2

EVENT   Etnies 20 Years

CLIENT   Etnies

DESIGN   Kira Evans Design

1

YOU AND A GUEST
ARE CORDIALLY INVITED TO JOIN
CULINARY ADVENTURES AND PERRIER-JOUËT
FOR THE UNVEILING OF

French 75 Bistro

— A SPECIAL EVENING BENEFITING SHARE OUR STRENGTH —

THURSDAY, FEBRUARY 23, 2006
7:00PM
3400 WEST OLIVE AVENUE · BURBANK

FOR INFORMATION CALL 323.262.7533
RSVP INFORMATION ENCLOSED

RSVP

FRENCH 75
BISTRO

CHAMPAGNE
PERRIER-JOUËT
Epernay - France

los angeles

YOU'RE INVITED TO CELEBRATE 20 YEARS OF ETNIES

20 etnies
Twenty Years

THREE CITIES
TWO DECADES
ONE RIDE

ETNIES SHOWROOM
29 GREENE STREET
NEW YORK, NEW YORK

THURSDAY, APRIL 6, 2006
9:00PM - 2:00AM

MONDAY, JUNE 12, 2006
10:00PM - 3:00AM

PALAIS DE TOKYO
13 AVENUE DU PRESIDENT WILSON
75116 PARIS FRANCE

NON-TRANSFERABLE.

MUSIC: ALDO (A1 RECORDS, NYC)
ED BANGER PARTY CRÜE:
PEDRO WINTER, DJ MEHDI, JUSTICE & SO ME
BIRDY NAM NAM SOUND SYSTEM
DJ PONE, LITTLE MIKE,
DJ NEED & CRAZY B

ADMISSION IS BY GUEST LIST ONLY.
INVITATION IS STRICTLY NON-TRANSFERABLE. PLEASE RSVP BY JUNE 6TH TO:
ETNIES20YEAR@SOLETECHNOLOGY.COM OR 310-979-1985

2

1 |
EVENT   NIRI Annual Conference
CLIENT   Internal
DESIGN   Thomson

2 |
EVENT   The Pearl at the Palms Casino
CLIENT   The Palms Casino and Resort
DESIGN   Kira Evans Design

1 |
EVENT   San Francisco Fashion Week
CLIENT   Erika Gessin
DESIGN   Hesselink Design

2 |
EVENT   The Boroughs Project
CLIENT   Timberland
DESIGN   Kira Evans Design

1

2

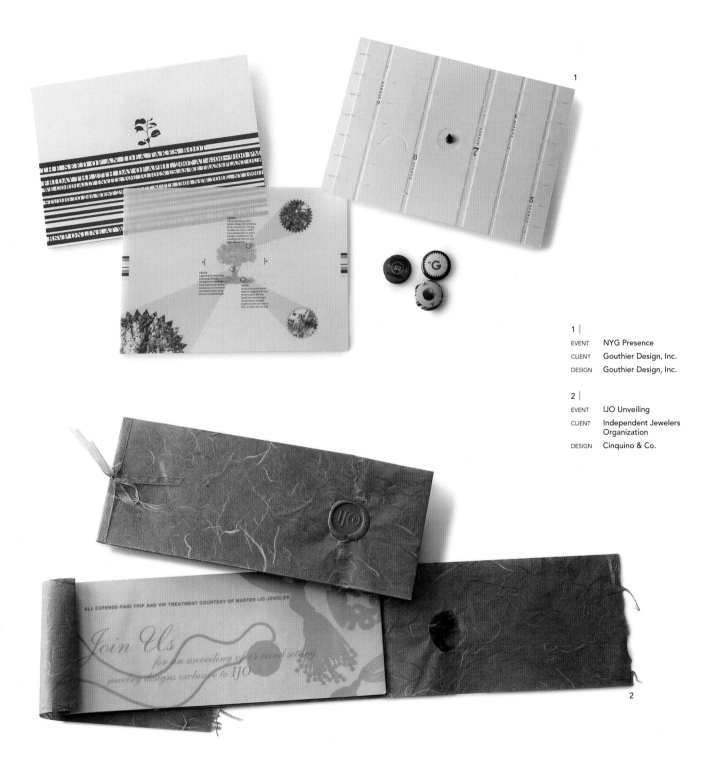

1 |

EVENT   NYG Presence

CLIENT   Gouthier Design, Inc.

DESIGN   Gouthier Design, Inc.

2 |

EVENT   IJO Unveiling

CLIENT   Independent Jewelers
Organization

DESIGN   Cinquino & Co.

1

1

EVENT   Trilix Tailgate
CLIENT   Trilix Marketing Group
DESIGN   Trilix Marketing Group

1

2

1 | 2 | 3 |
EVENT   Subplot Design, Inc. Launch
CLIENT   Subplot Design, Inc.
DESIGN   Subplot Design, Inc.

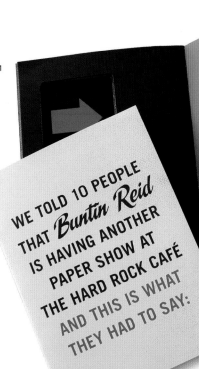

1

2

1 |
EVENT   Buntin Reid Paper Show
CLIENT Buntin Reid
DESIGN KOLEGRAM

2 |
EVENT   Iron Chef
CLIENT Orient Express Hotels
DESIGN THERE

World Pork Expo

Trilix Marketing Group

The World Pork Expo is an industry trade show and net-working event held annually for local, national, and international pork producers.

Produced by the National Pork Producers Council (NPPC), the event provides an opportunity for pork producers to meet with their allied industry clients and counterparts, preview new products, attend educational seminars, and network with others in the pork trade. Now in its 19th year, the event is always held at the Iowa State Fairgrounds in Des Moines. The 2007 expo was attended by 35,000 pork industry professionals (5,000 of whom were international attendees) and featured over 1,000 industry-related exhibits.

Trilix Marketing Group was charged with creating the advertising, promotion, and media relations for the World Pork Expo. They have developed a good working rapport with the NPPC as well as an efficient design and production process. The initial design concepts were developed in just three weeks and executed progressively over the months leading up to the event. With a budget of $35,000 for both design and production (including postage and signage), funds had to be used wisely.

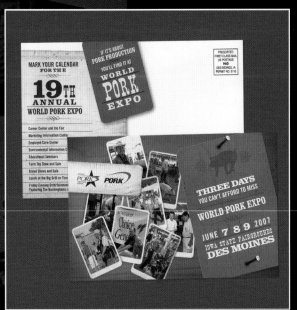

Trilix produced nearly all of the collateral materials, including 11,000 direct mail pieces, event signage, promotional materials, advertising, and website development, and maintenance. They took on a great

deal of work and responsibility, including strategic planning, design concepts, media planning, on-site media relations, and technical support. They began communicating with exhibitors early in the year, followed by international marketing and then national, regional, and local marketing outlets.

Trilix is faced with the challenge of making World Pork Expo visually come alive each year. For the 2007 event, they wanted to create a look and feel that was familiar and progressive, and appealed to both a business savvy, and rural clientele. They were also asked to incorporate photographs from the previous year's event. Taking all factors and viewpoints into account, Trilix developed a look for the campaign that was familiar, but still stylish and cool; a look they call "flea market chic." They used wood paneling as the backdrop for all of the pieces with other design elements "nailed" onto it. They also drew inspiration from block printing techniques for the type and graphic elements of the design. The combination of these two elements conjured memories of local, public gatherings with

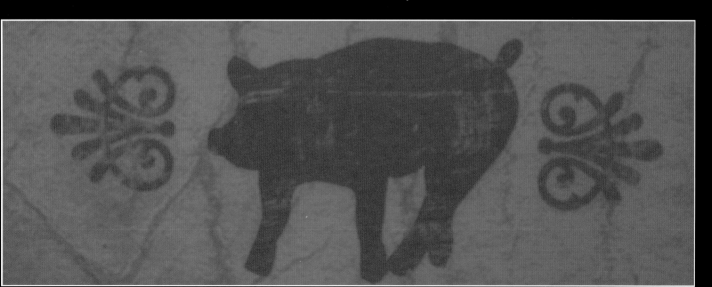

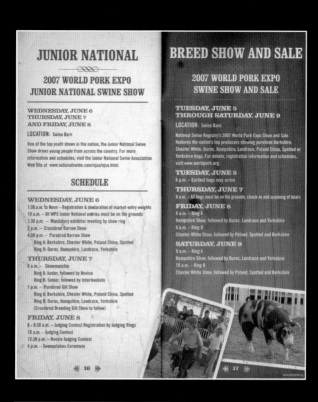

block-printed signs nailed on to public bulletin boards—an image that is certainly familiar to those who grew up in rural areas (as the majority of the attendees did).

The event's brand identity served as the jumping off point for each year's designs including the organization logo, event logo, and tagline. The agency then developed three suggested themes and/or design concepts. These concepts took into account client suggestions as well as any special circumstances, such as the Expo's upcoming 20th anniversary. Also, because the target audience is very narrow, Trilix focused its marketing goals from a consumer-based strategy to one that specifically targeted pork producers and event exhibitors.

Each element of the campaign, though cohesive and integrated, is visually strong enough to stand on its own. However, there were four main elements that had to be consistently applied. First was the "flea market chic" style conveyed with rough, wrinkled, and worn edges on elements within each piece. Second was the muted color palette reminiscent of faded photos. Third, was the layout that gave the impression that the elements within each piece had been haphazardly tossed onto a table. Finally, there was consistency created through the woodblock typographic style. Each of the elements are recognizable whether viewed together or as individual pieces.

1 | 2 |

EVENT   PACE 2007

CLIENT   PACE, SSPC, and PDCA

DESIGN   Bowhaus Design Groupe

1

2

1 |

EVENT   W Las Vegas Residences Lounge
at the Sundance Film Festival

CLIENT   W Las Vegas

DESIGN   Kira Evans Design

2 |

EVENT   Tao Las Vegas

CLIENT   Tao Restaurant

DESIGN   Kira Evans Design

1 |

EVENT   2003 Cape Town, South Africa

CLIENT   American Express Bank

DESIGN   Wing Chan Design, Inc.

2 |

EVENT   Great Achievers 2004 Santa Fe

CLIENT   American Express Bank

DESIGN   Wing Chan Design, Inc.

GREAT ACHIEVERS 2004

AMERICAN EXPRESS BANK

2

1

Great Achievers 2003

Cape Grace Hotel   Cape Town, South Africa
February 18-21, 2004

1 |
EVENT   *Blue-Gray Tournament*
CLIENT   The Olde Farm
DESIGN   The Bingham Group, Inc.

1
EVENT   Ritz Carlton Celebration
         of Caribbean Cuisine
CLIENT   The Ritz Carlton Hotels,
         Caribbean & Mexico
DESIGN   Gouthier Design: a brand collective

2
EVENT   Kean University Holiday Party
CLIENT   Kean University
DESIGN   The Design Studio at Kean University

1

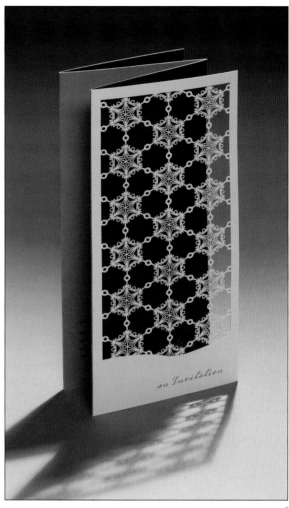

2

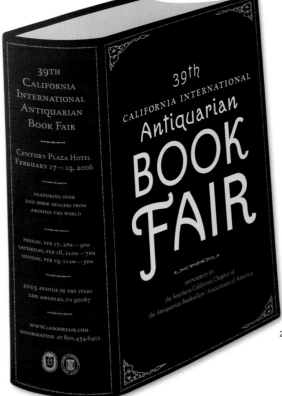

1 |

EVENT   El Rey Theatre Re-Grand Opening

CLIENT   Goldenvoice

DESIGN   Joven Orozco Design

2 |

EVENT   Antiquarian Book Fair

CLIENT   Southern CA Chapter of
         Antiquarian Booksellers
         Association of America

DESIGN   DISTINC

3 |

EVENT   Destination Fashion

CLIENT   MLC Centre—Jones Lang Lasalle

DESIGN   THERE

1 |

EVENT   ALA (American Library Association)
         Midwinter Meeting 2007

CLIENT   American Library Association

DESIGN   Innovative Interfaces

2 |

EVENT   Readymade Magazine's Winter Ball

CLIENT   Readymade magazine
         and Volume Design

DESIGN   The Small Stakes

1

2

1 |
EVENT   Reservoir Capital Annual
         Holiday Party
CLIENT   Reservoir Capital US Open
DESIGN   Synergy Graphix

2 |
EVENT   Leadership Team Awards
CLIENT   ERA
DESIGN   Kira Evans Design

1 |

EVENT   Autumn/Winter 2007
         Collection Preview
CLIENT   Bruno Grizzo
DESIGN   Matthias Ernstberger Design

1

BRUNO GRIZZO
CORDIALLY INVITES YOU
TO VIEW HIS THIRD
WOMENSWEAR COLLECTION
AUTUMN/WINTER 2007
AT W29 SHOWROOM,
NEW YORK.

1

EVENT   Nita B. Creative Open House
CLIENT   Nita B. Creative
DESIGN   Nita B. Creative

2

EVENT   Reactor Open House
CLIENT   Reactor
DESIGN   Reactor

FUND-RAISERS

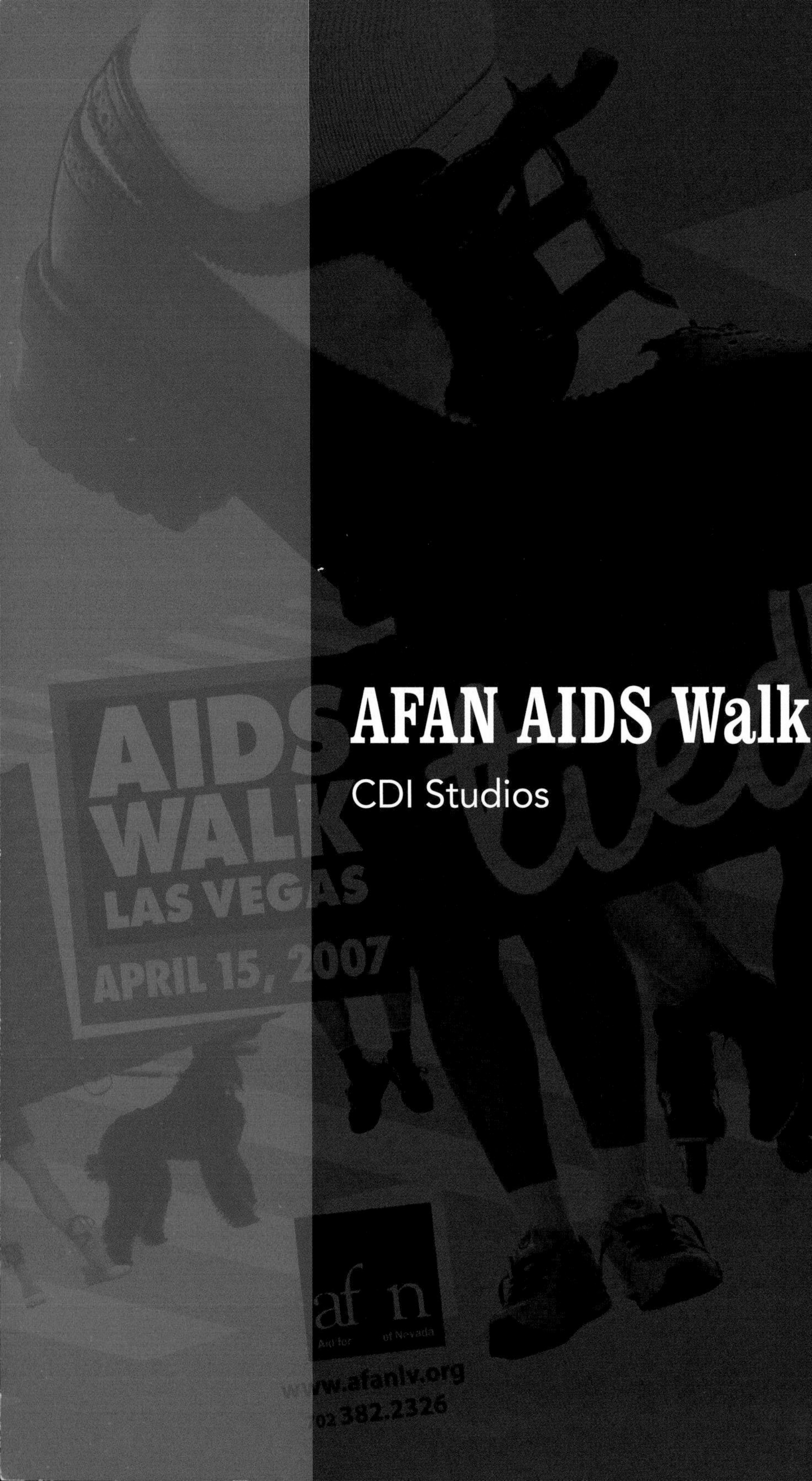

AFAN AIDS Walk

CDI Studios

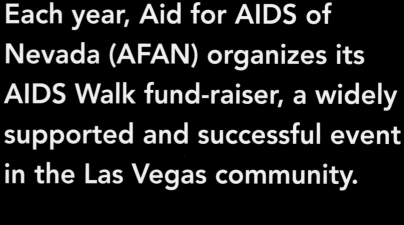

Each year, Aid for AIDS of Nevada (AFAN) organizes its AIDS Walk fund-raiser, a widely supported and successful event in the Las Vegas community.

In 2007, the event was emceed by Penn and Teller, the famed comedian-magicians and Las Vegas regulars, who served as a big draw for potential attendees. The event proved so successful that they far surpassed the $400,000 fund-raising goal by raising $520,000.

For the past five years, CDI Studios of Las Vegas has donated its services for the AFAN AIDS Walk fund-raisers, creating the concept, design, and producing all promotional materials. This included: registration and donation cards, brochures, postcards, print advertising campaigns, posters, signage, merchandise, and even a television ad. The design team wanted to create a fun and welcoming environment that would embrace and reach a diverse group of participants. They were able to accomplish this by creating yearly themes with a singular message of "collectivity."

Using the slogans, "Everyone Walks" and "Tied Together" and associateed imagery, CDI tried to communicate the idea that this

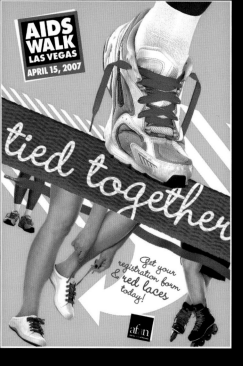

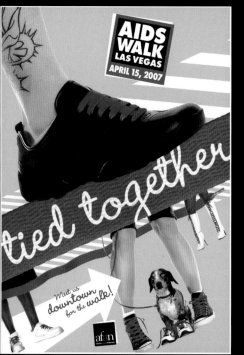

disease affects everyone and that the only way to combat it is to fight it collectively. Beginning with the 2004 walk, they used a pedestrian crosswalk "walking man" icon, which served as a way of connecting people through familiar imagery while reinforcing the message. Furthermore, by often showing the "walking man" on a backdrop of the Las Vegas strip, the imagery is grounded within the community, driving home the idea that this disease affects Las Vegas, too.

This "walking man" evolved over a five-year period, but feeling that it had run its course, in 2007, a new design focused on a new image of a series of people shown from the calf down wearing a variety of shoes tied with red laces, mimicking the red AIDS awareness ribbons. The campaign features a wide array of shoe types—everything from stiletto boots, to running shoes, to roller skates, and combat boots—symbolizing the diversity of people affected by HIV and AIDS and powerfully combined with the "Tied Together" slogan. Red shoelaces were also offered as a giveaway with the hope of creating a consistently recognizable symbol in the same vein as the rubber bracelets used by many nonprofit campaigns.

AIDS WALK
LAS VEGAS
APRIL 15, 2007
tied together
We're all tied together in the fight against AIDS!
who?
AIDS affects everyone!
HIV/AIDS affects the lives of everyone in our community in some way. We're all tied together in the fight against AIDS.
Aid for AIDS of Nevada (AFAN) provides support and advocacy for adults and children living with and affected by HIV/AIDS in southern Nevada. AFAN works to reduce HIV infection through prevention education to eliminate fear, prejudice and the stigma associated with the disease understanding, compassion and acceptance.
what?
It's Nevada's biggest event in the fight against AIDS!
Join Grand Marshals Penn & Teller, local celebrities, community leaders and local businesses in making this event a huge success. Through walker participation, corporate sponsorship, team support, and media coverage, the AIDS Walk raises funds and awareness to help those AFAN serves.
You can make a difference!
Last year many walkers raised thousands of dollars.
now at afanlv.org!
Lace up & Walk!
afan
WWW.AFANLV.ORG
TIED TOGETHER 2007 AFAN AIDS WALK

campaigns, allowing them the ability to fully explore themes and concepts. For the 2007 walk they created a cohesive campaign of materials by using consistent imagery, and colors that were inspired by the vintage Pee-Chee folders and the pop art movement. They also tried to give the images a cut and paste aesthetic in order to create a modern, urban feel. The largest challenge they faced was in creating the dynamic registration forms that included the red shoelaces, as these required a great deal of manual assembly. With the help of AFAN volunteers, they were able to put together nearly 15,000 units. This eye-catching element coupled with meaningful imagery created a dynamic evolution of the AFAN Aids Walk brand.

1 |

EVENT   Rumble to the River

CLIENT   THF

DESIGN   TOKY Branding + Design

2 |

EVENT   14th Annual Printmakers Ball

CLIENT   Anchor Graphics

DESIGN   Firebelly Design

3 |

EVENT   Death Cab for Cutie: A Hurricane
         Katrina Benefit Concert

CLIENT   Death Cab for Cutie

DESIGN   The Small Stakes

4 |

EVENT   Battle of the Bands

CLIENT   Portland Advertising Federation

DESIGN   Dotzero Design

5 | 6 | 7 |

EVENT   The Bird Carnival

CLIENT   The Bird Carnival

DESIGN   The Compound Design

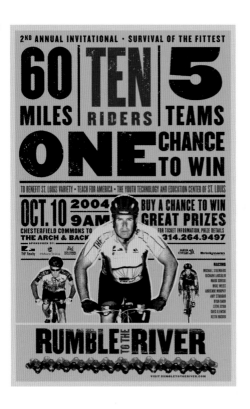

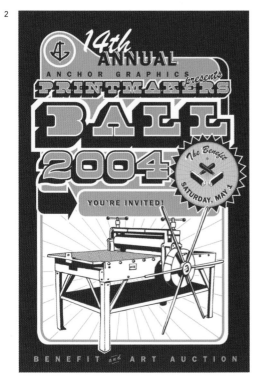

5

6

7

1 | 2 | 3 |

EVENT   JDRF Promise

CLIENT   Juvenile Diabetes
         Research Foundation

DESIGN   Juicebox Designs

EVENT   Opera Theatre Annual Gala

CLIENT   Opera Theatre of Saint Louis

DESIGN   TOKY Branding + Design

2

EVENT   A Tasteful Affair 19

CLIENT   Food Outreach

DESIGN   TOKY Branding + Design

1 |

EVENT   A Tasteful Affair 16

CLIENT   Food Outreach

DESIGN   TOKY Branding + Design

2 |

EVENT   Opera Theatre Annual Wine
         Tasting & Auction 2006

CLIENT   Opera Theatre of Saint Louis

DESIGN   TOKY Branding + Design

2

1

1

2

1 |

EVENT   Moonlight Masquerade Benefit

CLIENT   Lantern Theatre Company

DESIGN   gdloft

2 |

EVENT   Evening on the Bayou

CLIENT   Royal Caribbean &
Communities in School

DESIGN   Greteman Group

2

1

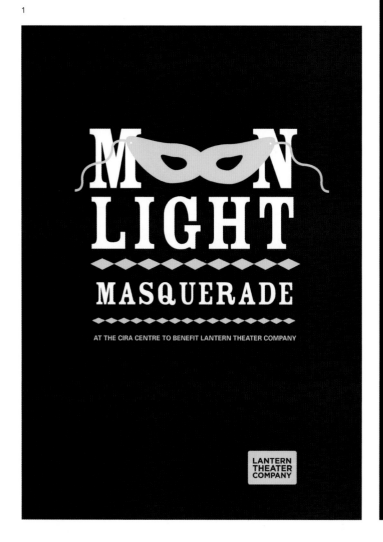

1

2

3

1 |

EVENT   Pajama Run

CLIENT   Community Action Team,
Long Beach, CA

DESIGN   Marc Posch Design, Inc.

2 |

EVENT   Long Beach Grunion Run

CLIENT   Community Action Team,
Long Beach, CA

DESIGN   Marc Posch Design, Inc.

3 |

EVENT   Haute Dog Easter Parade

CLIENT   Community Action Team,
Long Beach, CA

DESIGN   Marc Posch Design, Inc.

Avon Walk for Breast Cancer

Endless Possibilities Productions, Inc.

... 39-mile walk that takes place in several cities throughout the nation to raise money for breast cancer research.

The participants are mainly those who have been personally affected by breast cancer, either as survivors or loved ones of survivors and victims. This event seeks to bring these people together to share the experience and to work toward a common goal. The advertising and design campaign is focused on the participants, highlighting their commitment to the cause and solidarity with fellow walkers to raise funds and awareness for the fight against breast cancer.

Santa Monica–based design firm Endless Possibilities Productions, Inc. (EPOS) worked with JNR8 Advertising in 2004 and directly with Avon in 2005 to create a cohesive and effective brand identity that was both comforting and inspiring. Creative director Gabrielle Raumberger took an intuitive approach to the design process. By listening to the needs of the client and the goals of the project, she let her "creative intuition find the solution."

With just two weeks to submit the initial design concepts, the EPOS team came up with ten ideas that were narrowed down to a single final concept. Days later, a photo shoot was scheduled, cast, and completed, with the first ads going to press the following week.

such a short time frame for approvals and execution, the design team faced a significant challenge, especially when considering the vast size of the campaign. It included a four-part national ad campaign, counter displays, brochures, posters, postcards, direct mail, handbooks, T-shirts, invitations, forms, event signage, a website, and email blasts.

The look of the campaign was created by pairing a warm color palette with striking photography. The color pink, used throughout campaign materials, was coupled with a warm green meant to convey heart and healing. Photos by celebrity photographer Isabel Snyder captured both the vulnerability and spirit of the participants. She shot the participants on a well-lit, plain background in order to capture their true essence and glorify them and their contribution. For the second year, the photos were taken during the walk, as she literally pulled walkers off the path into the photography tent, capturing the walkers at their most vulnerable and determined.

Great Commitment:
Training and Fundraising

Great Cause

Great Need:
The Breast Cancer Epidemic

Great Bond

Great Bond

Great Charity: The Avon Foundation

Great Spirit

When was the last time

Great Weekend

Great Joy
(You better believe it!)

Great Outlook

HOPE.
TOGETHERNESS.
CELEBRATION.
TRIBUTE. BEAUTY.
AND A BLISTER OR TWO.

E AVON WALK

Non-Profit
Organization
U.S. Postage
PAID
Los Angeles, CA
Permit #1831

One weekend.

Great Crew

AVON WALK for BREAST CANCER

THERE ARE 52 WEEKS IN THE YEAR, BUT THERE'S ONLY
ONE WEEKEND!

AVONWALK.ORG 1-888-410-WALK

WELCOME TO
THE AVON WALK FOR BREAST CANCER
► Find out how Avon Foundation has been helping women since 19...

HOME   THE CAUSE   EVENT INFORMATION   TRIBUTES   EVENT NEWS   NEWSROOM   SIGN-IN

When was the last time you had a really great weekend?

WASHINGTON, DC MAY 1-2	SAN FRANCISCO JULY 10-11
BOSTON MAY 15-16	LOS ANGELES SEP 11-12
CHICAGO JUNE 5-6	NEW YORK OCT 2-3

Search This Site
FIND

Great Video!
See our latest TV Commerical.

Welcome to our newest National Sponsor

O NOVARTIS

► **REGISTER**
► **SUPPORT A WALKER/ CREW MEMBER**
► **REQUEST INFO**
► **TELL A FRIEND**
► **MY AVON WALK SIGN IN**
► **DONATE**
► **AVON WALK STORE**

The campaign was feminine, and dynamic, and sent a message that was full of optimism and humor. Its slogan began with the single word "great" used in conjunction with other terms to create message that were often funny, encouraging, or celebratory. On many T-shirt the slogan started with "great breasts" followed by one of a series of subheads such as, "saved by a mammogram," "I'm walking to save them," and "with great breasts comes great responsibility." Shirts designed for men read, "I'm a Breast Man walking for the cause." Over the next year, the campaign grew and shirts were designed with more hopeful messages, including "great courage," "great bond," "great hope," and "great weekend."

ARE YOU
READY FOR A
REALLY
GREAT...

...WEEK END?

AVON
WALK for
BREAST
CANCER
Avon Foundation is a
501(c)(3) public charity

The Avon Walk Weekend
is more than a walk for breast cancer. It's a breath of fresh air, a relief from the everyday, a release from the humdrum. It's your chance to dive headlong into what could be the most meaningful and rewarding weekend of your life.

Think of it. In a single triumphant span stretching from Saturday at dawn until Sunday afternoon, a few thousand spirited women and men in walking shoes and colorful hats will make a brash, beautiful statement the whole world will hear: "Breast Cancer is not the boss of us!"

It's a turning point in so many ways. Survivors proclaim their independence from the disease by marching strong, hand-in-hand. Loved ones participate to salute friends and relatives, and often walk beside them, giving back to the breast cancer community. Men and women who—as of yet—have no direct connection to breast cancer connect themselves by joining up with people who do.

We encourage you to get on the road today to a breast cancer-free tomorrow. **Register now and the experience begins!** Call **1-866-668-WALK** or visit **AVONWALK.ORG**

REGISTER OR DONATE TODAY · 1-866-668-WALK · AVONWALK.ORG

When viewed together, the 2004 and 2005 Avon Walk for Breast Cancer campaigns show a great deal of depth, courage, and growth. Starting in 2004 with a great concept, EPOS took a strong and comedic approach, eventually allowing it to develop into an equally strong, but more reverential and celebratory, message. With this message and an aesthetic that is at once bold, and feminine, vulnerable, and strong, EPOS created a vast array of materials that aptly represent the millions of women and men in this country affected by breast cancer and the organization dedicated to helping combat it.

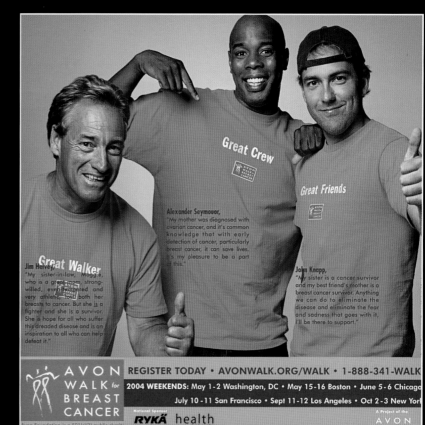

1

2

3

1 |

EVENT   16th Annual Harvest Celebration Ball

CLIENT   City of Hope

DESIGN   Kendall Ross

2 |

EVENT   First Night 2004

CLIENT   Grand Center

DESIGN   TOKY Branding + Design

3 |

EVENT   First Night 2005

CLIENT   Grand Center

DESIGN   TOKY Branding + Design

1

2

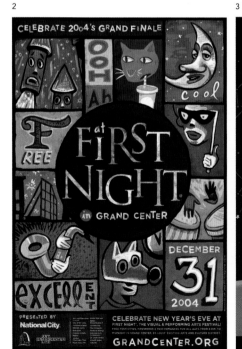

3

1 |
EVENT   One Enchanted Evening
CLIENT   City of Hope
DESIGN   Kendall Ross

Fonk Fest

Go Welsh

This event is all about the Fonk, a term used by John Gerdy, the president of Music for Everyone, who is known to describe things as being "so funky, it's FONKY."

When his organization set out to hold a fund-raiser to benefit music education, the path was clear. The festival design was going to have to be fun, creative, musical, and, of course, fonky. Go Welsh, a Lancaster County, Pennsylvania, design firm, donated its time and creative skills to make this fund-raising event live up to its fullest and fonkiest potential.

Gerdy started the Music for Everyone (MFE) organization to help restore music education in the Lancaster, Pennsylvania, area following funding cuts, with the belief that a good music education program would help to create "strong schools and vibrant communities." Since 2006, MFE has raised funds and awareness for this cause and has been able to provide several schools with instruments and money for continued music education. Its largest fund-raising effort to date was a two-day music festival held on a private farm in Conestoga, Pennsylvania, where several hundred attendees camped, ate, shared music and stories, and watched nearly fifteen different bands donate their performances. The wildly successful event exceeded all expectations, raising over $33,000.

Key to the success of the event was the support and design work provided by the Go Welsh team. By tapping in to what it really means to be "fonky," Go Welsh was able to create a campaign that was at once fun, whimsical, and exciting. They developed a color palette that was bright and energetic, but still comfortable and welcoming. They created illustrations that gave the feeling of paper cutouts, creating a handmade feel to the design work and mirroring the grassroots nature of the event itself. The illustrations developed into a representation of what one might expect to find at the festival itself: a funky musician, dancing partygoers (adult and child), a rabbit, a musical bird, and a "skonk" (the Fonk Fest interpretation of a skunk). Stark line drawings stood out against solid fields of color, or against solid color with a series of swirls and/or clouds.

The Fonk Fest design components included: invitations, email blasts, posters, wristbands, hats, T-shirts, price lists, event schedules, buttons, stationery, signage, and character cutouts. The design needed to be applied to all these components and had to engage and excite the audience while making them feel part of something special. In other words, the design had to be personal and approachable.

After exploring the possibility of taking a photographic approach, it was decided that illustrations would better capture the mood than would the photos of hippies that they continually encountered. But this came with its own set of challenges because the printing budgets were low and illustrations required a great deal of handcrafted work. The Go Welsh team spent a great deal of time and effort constructing

and painting a 3D sign of the event logo, which became a focal point for the event and tied the various pieces together. They also made large cutouts of the entire family of Fonk characters, placing them in the event space. A true testament to the success of the design came when people were spotted taking photographs with the Fonk family cutouts.

Aside from having donated their design efforts, Go Welsh also volunteered to staff Fonk Fest. Their whimsical designs set the tone for the event and created an enjoyable, lighthearted atmosphere, which contributed to the overall success of the event.

1

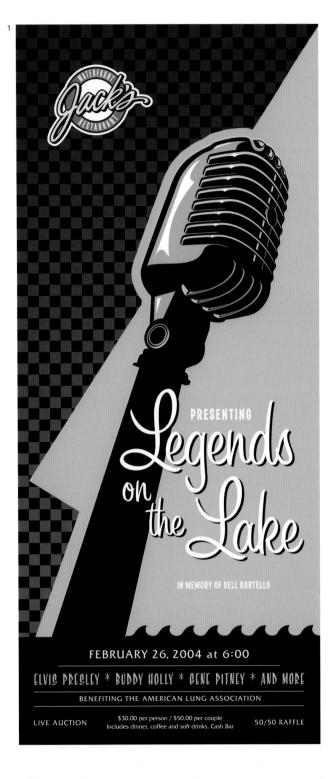

2

1 |
EVENT   Cattle Baron's Ball
CLIENT   J. Walter Thompson/ACS
DESIGN   RED Studios

1

2

3

4

5

6

7

1 |

EVENT   2006 Le Masquerade Gala

CLIENT   Phoenix Symphony

DESIGN   Bohnsack Design

2 |

EVENT   Wee Dream Ball

CLIENT   Rafanelli Events

DESIGN   Fresh Oil

3 |

EVENT   Jubilee Concert

CLIENT   The Norwalk Emergency Shelter

DESIGN   Tom Fowler, Inc.

4 |

EVENT   IslandWood Dinner in the Woods

CLIENT   IslandWood

DESIGN   View Design Company

5 |

EVENT   Race for the Cure 2007

CLIENT   Joven Orozco Design

DESIGN   Joven Orozco

6 |

EVENT   Heart Ball Detroit

CLIENT   Rafanelli Events

DESIGN   Fresh Oil

7 |

EVENT   Builders Ball

CLIENT   Habitat for Humanity

DESIGN   DISTINC

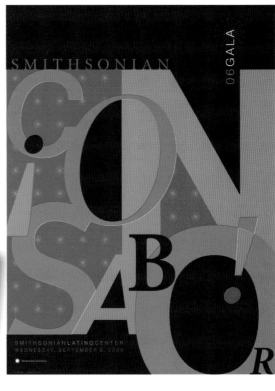

International Conference on Social Entrepreneurship in India
24th – 26th November 2006

at the Tata Institute of Social Sciences

1 | 2 | 3 |

EVENT   Smithsonian Latino
             Center 2006 Gala

CLIENT   Smithsonian Latino Center

DESIGN   Grafik Marketing
             Communication

4 | 5 | 6 | 7 |

EVENT   Social Entrepreneurship
             Conference in India

CLIENT   UnLtd UK

DESIGN   UMS Design Studio

1 |

EVENT   Painted Pony Ball

CLIENT   St. Francis Children's Hospital

DESIGN   Walsh Associates

2 |

EVENT   2002 Imagine Awards Gala

CLIENT   Inner-City Arts

DESIGN   DISTINC

1

2

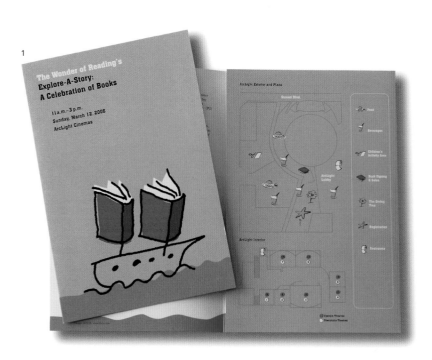

The High Museum Atlanta Wine Auction

The Jones Group

The High Museum of Art in Atlanta, Georgia, is the leading art museum in the southeastern United States.

Since 1993, the museum has held the High Museum Atlanta Wine Auction (HMAWA) to support museum acquisitions, exhibitions, and educational programming. This wine auction ranks as one of the top five charity wine auctions in the country, attracting some of the most prominent winemakers from the U.S. and abroad. The event also hosts international wine experts and special guests from California's Napa Valley. Ensuring its success, 100 vintners donated 200 auction lots, which, over the last fourteen years, have amounted to over $10 million dollars, $1.8 million of which was raised in 2007 alone.

In 2005, The Jones Group of Atlanta, Georgia, was brought in to brand the event with a unique visual look and personality. The scope of the project included invitations, posters, a website, brochures, gala program catalog, lot numbers, auction displays, bidding paddles, and nametags. They also created a number of promotional materials including hats, tote bags, aprons, T-shirts, and etched wine glasses. In developing the design to be applied to all of these materials, they had to take into account the very select group of people that they were trying to reach. In this case, they were trying to entice both

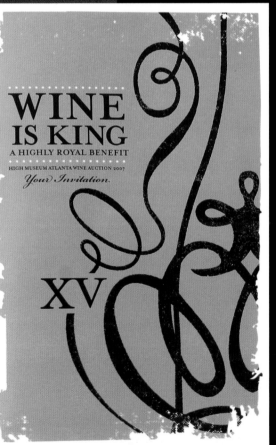

international wineries and those on the West Coast to donate their prized vintages for the fund-raising auction. They also had to appeal to local wine lovers who would attend the event and bid on the donated items.

The Jones Group developed a brand identity that would appeal to their target audience, could be carried through the production of various materials, and captured the spirit of the High Museum and the event itself. They branded everything from the invitations, and websites, to wine glasses, and the actual dance floor. The challenge was individualizing each piece while still ensuring that it felt like part of the larger brand identity of the event. The final design contained elements that could be extracted to stand alone while still maintaining a recognizable connection to the whole.

Each year, the High Museum Wine Auction organizing committee and cochairs developed a new theme for the event. The theme was often determined by a museum expansion, an important exhibit, or a milestone anniversary for the museum or the event. 2007 marked a special year for the HMAWA; it was not only the fifteenth anniversary of the event, but was the year that the museum partnered with the Louvre in Paris on a special exhibition from Louis XV's personal collection titled, "Kings as Collectors." Thus was born the theme, "Wine Is King," which embodied the longevity of the wine auction and the royal nature of this special exhibit. The design included regal imagery including a throne, crown, and "XV" mark, as well as a wine bottle and a series of ribbonlike flourishes that added a bit of flare

in the royal colors of purple and blue to accentuate the majestic connection. The design was carried through to the event space with purple lighting and accents, and the imagery of the bottle, crown, and flourishes displayed everywhere from the stage floor to projections on the tent walls.

The success of the High Museum Atlanta Wine Auction was its ability to bring together exquisite wines, chefs, and vintners with an affluent body of museum supporters and wine connoisseurs. The Jones Group's design gave this event a sophisticated look while maintaining a fun, classy atmosphere.

1 |
EVENT   Concert of Compassion
CLIENT   St. Luke's United Methodist Church
DESIGN   Funnel

2 |
EVENT   LA Open
CLIENT   Community Action Team,
          Long Beach, CA
DESIGN   Marc Posch Design, Inc.

1

2

1 |
EVENT   Arts Desire 05
CLIENT   Contemporary Art
         Museum St. Louis
DESIGN   TOKY Branding + Design

1 |

EVENT   Benefit Concert 2006:
         Kids Helping Kids

CLIENT   Belmont Hill School

DESIGN   Jenn David Design

1

1 |

EVENT   Brent Bolthouse's Birthday

CLIENT   Smashbox

DESIGN   Kira Evans Design

2 |

EVENT   ARTS DESIRE The Art
          and Wine Auction

CLIENT   The Contemporary Art
          Museum St. Louis

DESIGN   TOKY Branding + Design

1 |
EVENT   An Evening in Paris
CLIENT   Koret Family House
DESIGN   Jenny Duarte Graphic Design

2 | 3 |
EVENT   The Bang on a Can Benefit Party
CLIENT   Bang on a Can
DESIGN   Another Limited Rebellion

4 |
EVENT   Magical Moments
CLIENT   The Heinzerling Foundation
DESIGN   Element

1

2

3

4

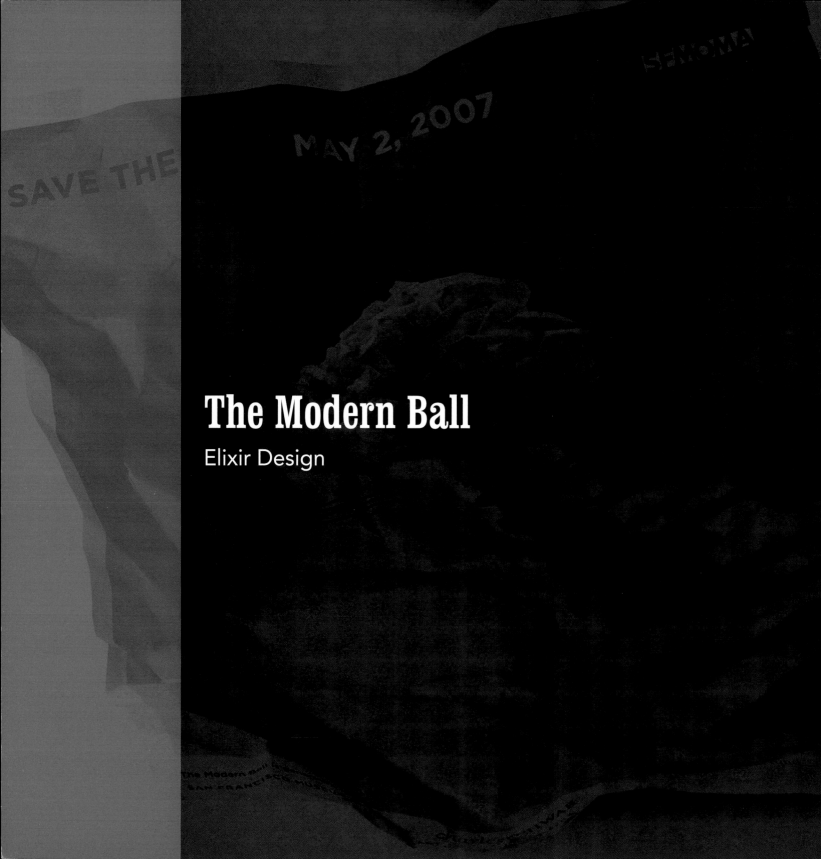

The Modern Ball

Elixir Design

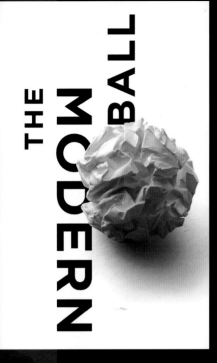

In 2005, the San Francisco Museum of Modern Art (SFMOMA) inaugurated the Modern Ball, a biennial fund-raiser held to raise money for the museum's exhibitions and education programs.

Since the museum's inception in 1995, this event has been its largest fund-raiser. Famed event designer Stanlee Gatti designed this "chic, creative and glamorously social evening." The benefit included a formal dinner for corporate sponsors and large contributors, a lounge-style party for a younger crowd, and the Post-Modern Ball, a late-night after party. Because the ultimate goal of the event was to raise funds for the museum, the event mirrored the museum's personality, the creativity of its exhibits, and the diversity of the attendees, creating a truly memorable and unique experience.

San Francisco–based Elixir Design designed the identity and various print and web–based design elements in support of the Modern Ball. They worked closely with Gatti and the Modern Ball Committee to develop a look and feel that would not only brand the first event but that could maintain a core identity while evolving each year.

Taking into consideration the large scope of the project (an identity system, press kit, stationery, advertising, promotional postcards, save-the-date, invitation, programs, flash emails, website link and desktop wallpaper), Elixir's goal was to create an identity that would be cohesive not only when seen together, but also when set across the backdrop of the museum and its own branding.

The logo for the event retained the simple color field and bold, vertical type found in the SFMOMA logo, but playfully oriented the text vertically and altered the directions of each word. Elixir also used the word ball as inspiration, incorporating an image of a ball that could be altered in future designs and playing with the terminology and imagery in a very artful, contemporary fashion. Elixir drew inspiration from some of the prolific artists found on the museum's own walls, including Ed Ruscha, John Baldessari, and Claes Oldenburg, to determine what type of ball would be used for a given year. The photography of Melvin Sokolosky was also a notable influence in the design of the 2007 save-the-dates.

A key element to the success of the event was creating buzz and media attention well before the event took place, making the save-

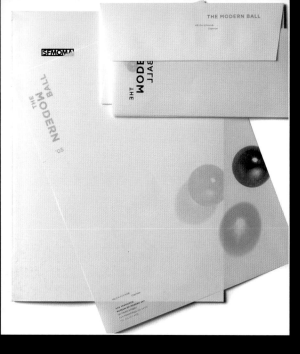

the-date pieces particularly important in setting the tone for the rest of the imagery. In 2005, the save-the-dates pictured a sphere reminiscent of a planet or the solar system. But the 2007 piece took the design to a new level. Lucky invitees received a white box wrapped with a blue band labeled, "The Modern Ball." Inside the box was a clear, plastic sphere with a crumpled save-the-date inside that featured the same image of a crumpled piece of paper in a perfect sphere on a soothing blue color field. This crumpled but perfect circular ball and the introduction of a second color served as the changing elements in the 2007 Modern Ball identity. Finding the perfect plastic sphere was a difficult task for Elixir, but it proved to be a successful and effective piece.

While the Modern Ball is a new fund-raising endeavor for the SFMOMA, it raised over $1.7 million dollars in its inaugural year alone. Much of the event's success lies in the successful and fruitful collaboration between Elixir Design and the Modern Ball committee. Having a strong working relationship and foundation to build upon, Elixir was able to create a fresh, interesting, and effective design.

THE
MODERN
BALL

'07

SFMOMA
SAN FRANCISCO
MUSEUM OF MODERN ART
151 THIRD STREET
SAN FRANCISCO, CA 94103

THE MODERN BALL

ELAINE McKEON
Chair

SAN FRANCISCO
MUSEUM OF MODERN ART
151 THIRD STREET
SAN FRANCISCO, CA 94103
TEL 415-357-4136

COMMUNITY & EDUCATION

1

2

1 |

EVENT   Ski Seminar 2004

CLIENT   DENTSPLY Tulsa Dental
          Specialties

DESIGN   David Clark Design

1 | 2 |

EVENT   Ski Seminar 2005

CLIENT   DENTSPLY Tulsa Dental
          Specialties

DESIGN   David Clark Design

1

2

3

1 |

EVENT   2007 Dubuque …and All That Jazz
Outdoor Jazz Concert Series

CLIENT   Dubuque Main Street

DESIGN   Refinery Design Company

2 |

EVENT   2006 Dubuque …and All That Jazz
Outdoor Jazz Concert Series

CLIENT   Dubuque Main Street

DESIGN   Refinery Design Company

3 |

EVENT   2005 Dubuque …and All That Jazz
Outdoor Jazz Concert Series

CLIENT   Dubuque Main Street

DESIGN   Refinery Design Company

1 |

EVENT   Helvetica Movie Premiere

CLIENT   Helvetica the Movie

DESIGN   Pratt Institute

2 |

EVENT   25th Annual Oktoberfest

CLIENT   The MainStrasse Village
Association

DESIGN   Schilling Design

1

Featuring ERIK SPIEKERMANN,
NORM, JONATHAN HOEFLER,
EXPERIMENTAL JETSET, WIM
CROUWEL, MICHAEL BIERUT,
APFEL, PIERRE MIEDINGER,
HERMANN ZAPF, MATTHEW
CARTER, NEVILLE BRODY,
STEFAN SAGMEISTER, LARS
MULLER, MICHAEL C. PLACE,
BRUNO STEINERT, OTMAR
HOEFER, RICK POYNOR,
MASSIMO VIGNELLI, TOBIAS
FRERE-JONES, and many more

HELVETICA
EVERYWHERE MARCH 3 2007

A SWISS DOTS PRODUCTION
Produced and Directed by GARY
HUSTWIT. Editor SHELBY
SIEGEL. Sound Recordists
NARA GARBER, DAN JOHNSON,
VICTOR HORSTINK, SAM PULLEN,
JORG KIDOWSKI. Additional
Photography CHRIS WETTON,
GARY HUSTWIT, BEN WOLF
Director of Photography LUKE
GEISSBUHLER. Production
Assistance AMY HARRINGTON,
TYRONE BRAITHWAITE

1 | 2 |

EVENT   Read Romp + Rock
CLIENT   Rafanelli Events
DESIGN   Fresh Oil

1

2

1

2

3

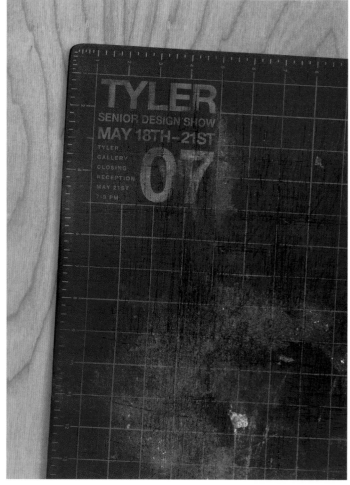

1 |
EVENT   Festivus
CLIENT   Various
DESIGN   25projects.com

1

1 | 2 | 3 | 4 | 5 | 6 |

EVENT   Cesar Millan Webinars
CLIENT   Dog Psychology Center
DESIGN   Copia Creative, Inc.

1

Cesar has announced his topic two and topic three dates for his exclusive online webinars. Your ticket is confirmed for **Sunday, June 24th**. Cesar is looking forward to spending Sunday with you and addressing his long awaited topics. We appreciate your patience during this time and are happy to share the confirmed date with you.

SUNDAY, JUNE 24th

TOPIC 2 begins 11am PST (2pm EST)
TOPIC 3 begins 2pm PST (5pm EST)

No further action needs to be taken on your part. **We will notify you with login instructions a few days in advance.** We are really looking forward to these webinars as we are adding some special features and Cesar will be live from the DPC direct to your home.

We will see you there!

Topic 2:
Learning and Addressing Problem Behaviors

Topic 3:
Your Energy, Your Dog

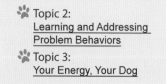
www.cesarmillanwebinars.com

2

1 | 2 | 3 |

EVENT   Mercy Gilber Medical Center
           Grand Opening

CLIENT   Catholic Healthcare West

DESIGN Campbell Fisher Design

1

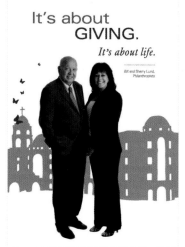

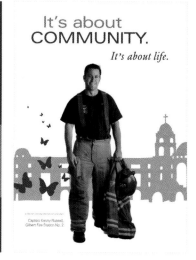

2

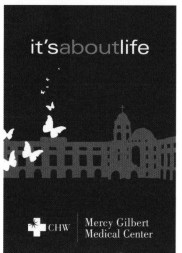

3

1 | 2 |
EVENT   Scoot-A-Que 9
CLIENT   Columbus Cutters Scooter Club
DESIGN   Element

1 |

EVENT   Dedication of the Homestead
         National Monument of America
         Heritage Center
CLIENT   Friends of Homestead
DESIGN   Archrival

2 |

EVENT   2005 Wellness Fair
CLIENT   Shoreline Community College
DESIGN   Aaron Preciado Design

2

1

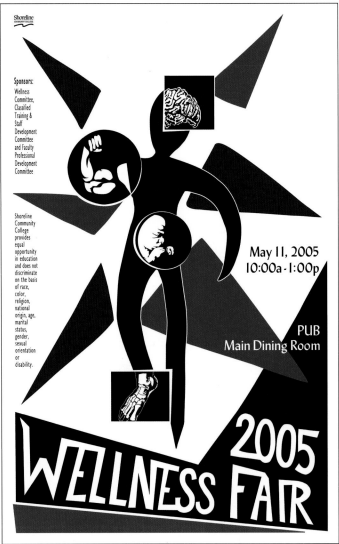

1

EVENT   Jr. Graphic Design Show,
          Class of 2007

CLIENT   Long Beach State

DESIGN   Elaine Inspired

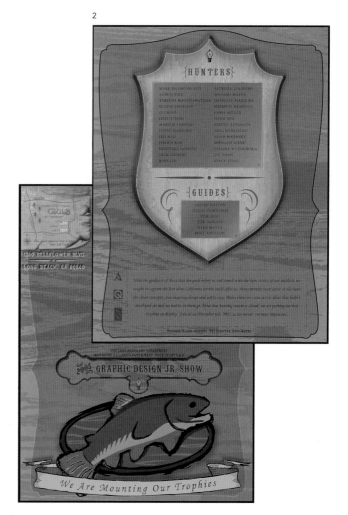

2

1 |

EVENT   Northside Independence Day
         Parade and Festival

CLIENT   Northside Business Association
         and Northside Community Council

DESIGN   Tricia Bateman

2 |

EVENT   Diversity at MIT Lecture Series

CLIENT   Massachusetts Institute
         of Technology

DESIGN   AdamsMorioka, Inc.

1

2

1 | 2 | 3 |
EVENT   FrightTown
CLIENT   FrightTown
DESIGN   Dotzero Design

1

2

3

Creative Future 2007

UMS Design

In 2007, the British Council of India began a program called Creative Future, the goal of which was to identify and nurture India's most promising young creative entrepreneurs with exciting business ideas.

After a nationwide search, twenty young people were selected to take part in the Creative Future School at the Indian Institute of Management in Bangalore. At the final Awards Nite the student with the most viable and creative business plan was given India's Creative Future 2007 award.

UMS Design Studio of Mumbai, India, designed all visual communication materials for the event. They worked closely with the British Council event project manager to develop the overall branding and look of the event and were charged with the design of posters and banners, invitations, a souvenir book, the stage design, and an animation to be played at the awards event. Part of the challenge of designing for this

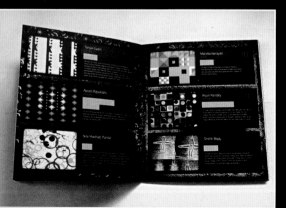

event was that it was geared toward the creative industry, so it would have to have to be interesting, original, and of impeccable quality. With that in mind, UMS set out to make something that on one level was simple and witty, but on another level was detailed and intense. Innovation and thoughtfulness were key to this development.

To accomplish this two-pronged approach to the design, UMS made a number of considered design choices. They chose to use only two colors: a vibrant, energetic yellow deeply contrasted with a stark black. An image of a butterfly was selected as a main design element representing the beautiful transformation and newfound ability to take flight that these honorees experience. However, the designers chose to merge two different images of a butterfly—one an ornate illustration, and the other a more pixel-based structure. These unlike pairings symbolized the duality of thought and talent possessed by these creative and business-savvy young entrepreneurs. Finally, a die-cut was used in the booklet to give added dimension and life to the design as well as lend additional meaning to the butterfly symbolism.

In addition to a die cut of the butterfly on the front cover, there is also a full page of butterfly die cuts within the book, each with a photo of one of the honorees visible behind it. The clever use of this production technique gave added meaning to the chosen imagery, as the butterfly seems to be literally taking flight from the page.

The design for the Creative Future program and Awards Nite set out to use symbolic, thought-provoking imagery, and unique production elements to create a campaign that was innovative, imaginative, and impressive. The audience for the event would include India's leading entrepreneurs and professionals from the visual arts, architecture, fashion, film, performing arts, interactive software, and gaming fields. The guests represented some of India's finest business and creative minds so the design had to reach and far surpass their expectations. In just five weeks, UMS Design Studio created a campaign of eye-catching and intelligent materials that aptly and elegantly represented this important educational endeavor.

1

2

EVENT   A Monumental Affair
CLIENT   Keep Indianapolis Beautiful
DESIGN   Funnel

1 |
EVENT   Fall Forum 2005
CLIENT   Coalition of Essential Schools
DESIGN   MINE

2 |
EVENT   Fall Forum 2006
CLIENT   Coalition of Essential Schools
DESIGN   MINE

1

2

1

admit one

1 |
EVENT   GKI Monrovia
         Christmas Concert
CLIENT   GKI Monrovia
DESIGN   HA Design

2 |
EVENT   San Francisco Fashion Week
CLIENT   Erika Gessin
DESIGN   Hesselink Design

2

1 |

EVENT   13th Tokyo International
         Book Fair 2006

CLIENT   SILNT

DESIGN   SILNT

2 |

EVENT   National Novel Writing Month

CLIENT   National Novel Writing Month

DESIGN   The Small Stakes

1

2

1 |
EVENT   All Hale, Jazz in June
CLIENT   K-State Friends of the Libraries
DESIGN   S&N Design

2 |
EVENT   CSG Alumnae Weekend
CLIENT   Columbus School for Girls
DESIGN   Element

1 |

EVENT   Tulsa Zoo Waltz on the
         Wild Side

CLIENT   Tulsa Zoo Friends

DESIGN   David Clark Design

2 |

EVENT   King Tut National Tour
         Media Event

CLIENT   AEG/Concerts West,
         National Geographic

DESIGN   Morris! Communication

1

2

3

4

5

1 |

EVENT   Growth Trends
CLIENT   ACG San Diego
DESIGN   Incitrio design{brand}media

2 |

EVENT   Flower Presentation
CLIENT   Floristik Schau Dortmund
DESIGN   CHSC design

3 |

EVENT   Bendigo Agricultural Show
CLIENT   Bendigo Agricultural
          Show Society
DESIGN   Dale Harris

4 |

EVENT   East Village Bike Night
CLIENT   East Village
DESIGN   Sayles Graphic Design

5 |

EVENT   Debonair Fish Affair
CLIENT   The Maritime Aquarium
          at Norwalk
DESIGN   Tom Fowler, Inc.

1 | 2 | 3 | 4 | 5 |
EVENT   Always Oxford St.
CLIENT   City of Sydney
DESIGN   THERE

4

5

1 | 2 | 3 |

EVENT   Bal Vividha
CLIENT   Comet Media Foundation
DESIGN   UMS Design Studio

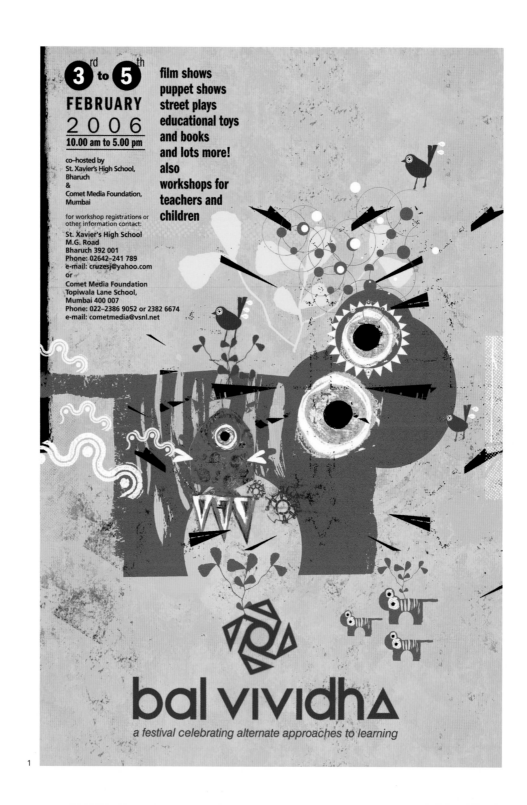

1

2

3

1 | 2 |

EVENT   International School Award
CLIENT   British Council, India
DESIGN   UMS Design Studio

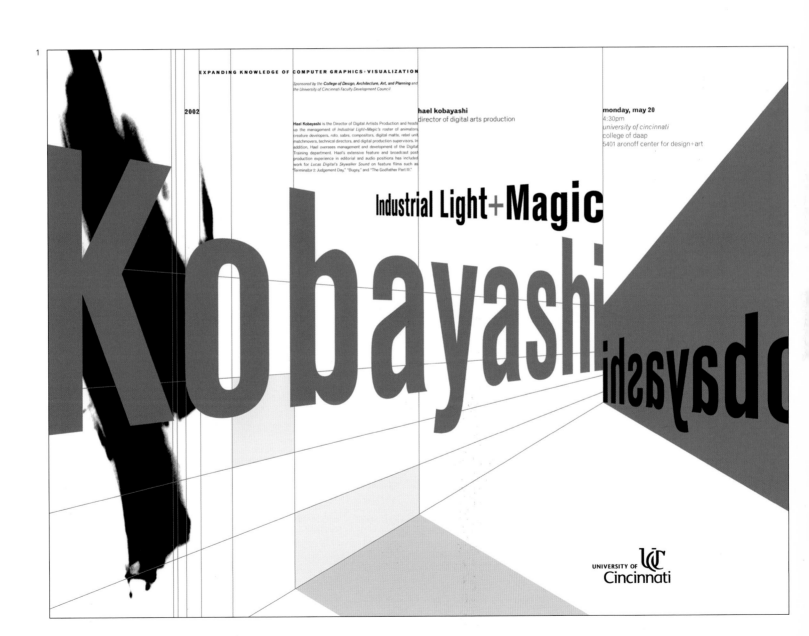

SAN FRANCISCO RISING

365 Mendell Street
San Francisco, CA 94124

The Call–Chronicle–Examiner

SAN FRANCISCO, THURSDAY, APRIL 19, 1906.

EARTHQUAKE AND FIRE:
SAN FRANCISCO IN RUINS

100 YEARS LA

1906 - 2006

MAYOR GAVIN NEWSOM
and
CHIEF OF PROTOCOL CHARLOTTE MAILLIARD SHULTZ
together with
SAN FRANCISCO RISING FINANCE CHAIRS
CHRIS AND LISA GRUWELL
and
SAN FRANCISCO RISING PHOENIX CIRCLE CHAIRS
RALPH AND CHERYL BAXTER
warmly invite you to

2

SAN FRANCISCO RISING
1906 EARTHQUAKE AND
FIRE COMMEMORATION

100 YEARS LATER

Join Mayor Gavin Newsom in celebrating
the enduring spirit of the City of San Francisco

Traditional Memorial at Lotta's Fountain on Tuesday, April 18 at 4:30 am
(Market & Kearny Streets)

Other Centennial Event Information: **sfrising.org** *Emergency Preparedness:* **72hours.org**

1 | 2 |

EVENT   San Francisco Rising
CLIENT   The City of San Francisco
DESIGN   Elixir Design

 ENTERTAINMENT

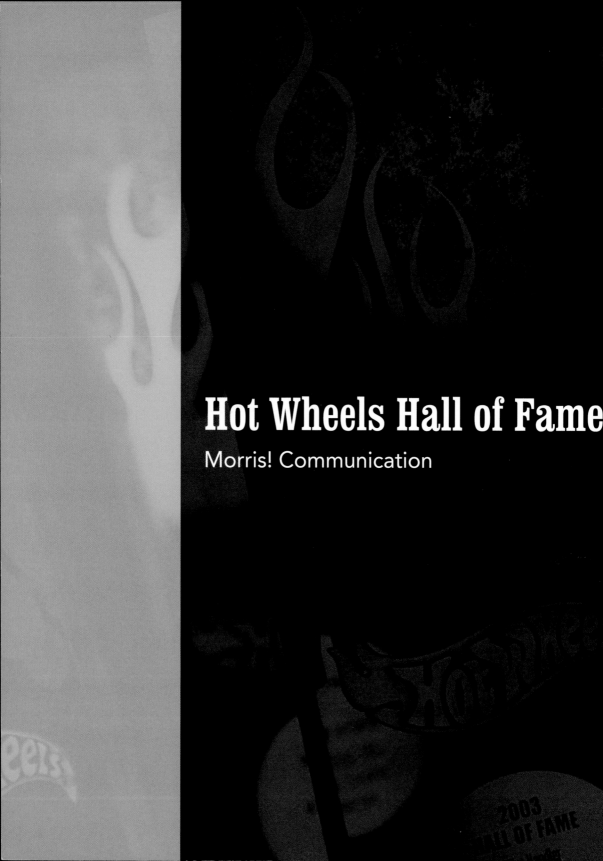

Hot Wheels Hall of Fame

Morris! Communication

inaugural inductees into the Hot Wheel Hall of Fame held at the Petersen Automotive Museum and emceed by the *Tonight Show*'s Jay Leno.

The event was the culmination of a wide-ranging marketing effort to strengthen the lifestyle positioning of the Hot Wheels brand as well as the grand opening of a permanent Hot Wheels exhibit at the museum showcasing the brand's impact on popular car culture and its relevance to the adult target market.

Steven Morris of Morris! Communication worked alongside the internal Hot Wheels brand team for five months prior to the event to develop a ballot package, invitations, event graphics, and an award statue.

Because the audience for this event would include legendary automotive VIPs, toy aficionados, entertainment industry executives, and the media, the design would have to embody the speed, power, performance, and attitude of the Hot Wheels brand but with a level of sophistication befitting a Hall of Fame ceremony. With this in mind, Morris began by developing the ballot package that would go out to a panel of auto journalists, manufacturers, designers, drivers, and Mattel (Hot Wheels parent company) executives. Morris designed a leather-bound portfolio enclosed in a brushed-steel, logo-embossed box. The package was sophisticated, dynamic, and received immediate praise from such car enthusiasts as Jay Leno, Richard Petty, and the heads of design at Ford and General Motors.

Equally impressive were the 1000 gala invitations Morris produced, each containing a die-cast Hot Wheels vehicle made for the event. Allowing the giveaway to be the focal point of the piece, he placed the invitation in a box with the event details printed on the side flaps. The invitations had an impressive response rate and immediately became a hot item in the fanatical Hot Wheels collector market.

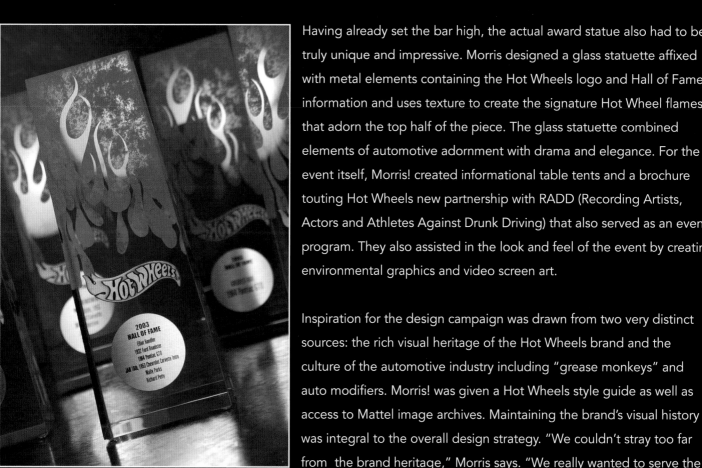

2003
HALL OF FAME
Elliot Handler
1932 Ford Roadster
1964 Pontiac GTO
JAN 16th, 1953 Chevrolet Corvette Intro
Wally Parks
Richard Petty

Having already set the bar high, the actual award statue also had to be truly unique and impressive. Morris designed a glass statuette affixed with metal elements containing the Hot Wheels logo and Hall of Fame information and uses texture to create the signature Hot Wheel flames that adorn the top half of the piece. The glass statuette combined elements of automotive adornment with drama and elegance. For the event itself, Morris! created informational table tents and a brochure touting Hot Wheels new partnership with RADD (Recording Artists, Actors and Athletes Against Drunk Driving) that also served as an event program. They also assisted in the look and feel of the event by creating environmental graphics and video screen art.

Inspiration for the design campaign was drawn from two very distinct sources: the rich visual heritage of the Hot Wheels brand and the culture of the automotive industry including "grease monkeys" and auto modifiers. Morris! was given a Hot Wheels style guide as well as access to Mattel image archives. Maintaining the brand's visual history was integral to the overall design strategy. "We couldn't stray too far from the brand heritage," Morris says. "We really wanted to serve the

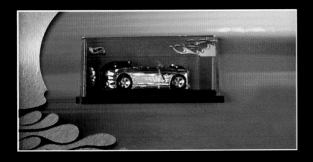

history well. It was billed as a hall of fame for die-cast vehicles, but in reality was much more than that. It honored the real cars that the toys emulate. It was really about honoring the source that Hot Wheels was built from." Morris adds, "The way that people adorned these vehicles had a lot to do with our inspiration, even tattoo culture. And it's a multisensory thing—the feel of grease, the smell of gasoline all contributed to the overall aesthetic."

Morris channeled these elements into each piece, using metal and metal–like elements whenever possible to establish the clear connection to the chrome found in automotive detailing. He referenced leather automotive interiors by creating a leather portfolio for the ballot packaging. Finally, he relied heavily on the iconic flame imagery found in both classic and Hot Wheels cars.

Although the brand is kid–targeted, it has a sizable number of adult collectors, so the design had to reflect a sophistication and seriousness while maintaining a youthful energy. The permanent museum display and every component of the star-studded orange-carpet event exemplified and amplified the deep-seated ties between Americans and their cars.

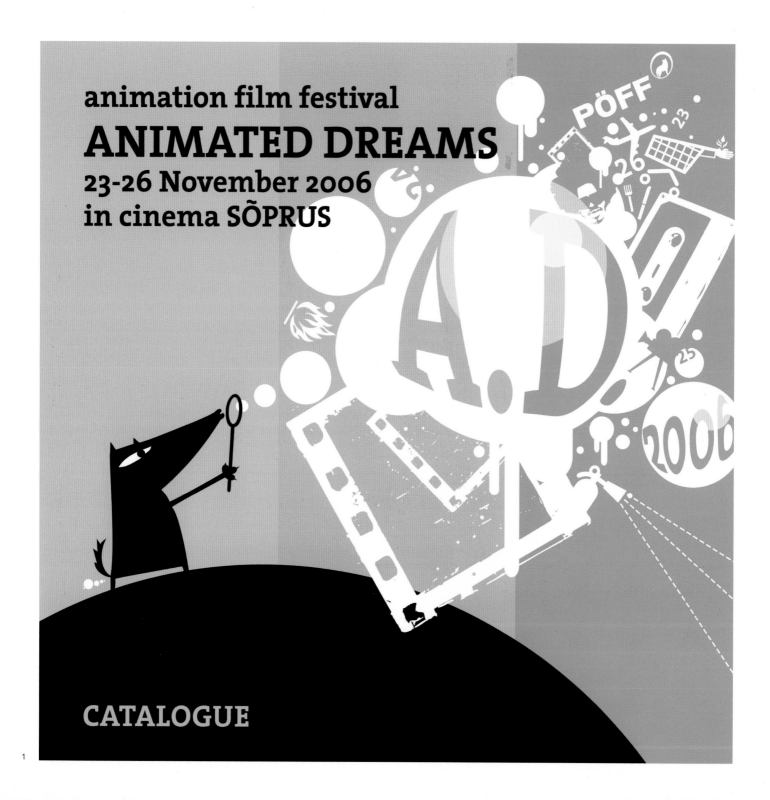

animation film festival

ANIMATED DREAMS

23-26 November 2006
in cinema SÕPRUS

CATALOGUE

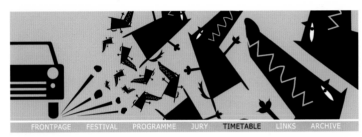

2

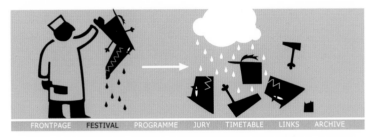

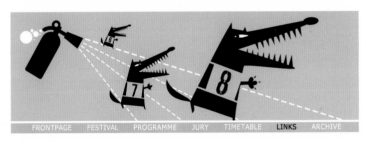

3

1 | 2 | 3 |

EVENT   Animated Dreams
CLIENT   Black Nights Film Festival
DESIGN   Anne Pikkov

1 |

EVENT   5th Annual Exhibition for
         Strategy and Fantasy

CLIENT   Strategy and Fantasy
         Games Club of Thessaloniki

DESIGN   Elixirion Design

2 |

EVENT   Nomad Foreign Film Series:
         Revenge

CLIENT   Nomad Lounge

DESIGN   Archrival

3 |

EVENT   Nomad Foreign Film Series:
         Bollox

CLIENT   Nomad Lounge

DESIGN   Archrival

1

2
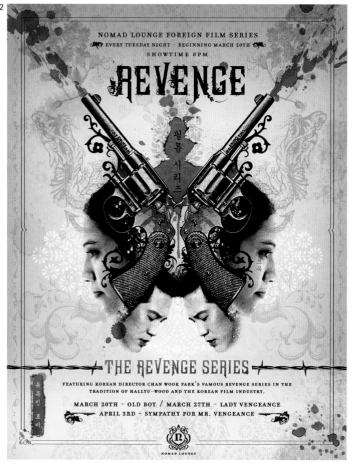

3

1

2

3

4

5

6

1 |
EVENT   U.S. Comedy Arts Festival
CLIENT   HBO
DESIGN   Tornado Design

2 |
EVENT   A Masked Ball
CLIENT   The Connecticut Grand
         Opera & Orchestra
DESIGN   Tom Fowler, Inc.

3 |
EVENT   TriBeCa Film Festival 2006
CLIENT   New York Times
DESIGN   Michael Doret/Alphabet Soup

4 |
EVENT   Mt. Hood Jazz Festival
CLIENT   Mt. Hood Jazz Festival
DESIGN   Dotzero Design

5 |
EVENT   Mill Valley Film Festival
CLIENT   Mill Valley Film Festival
DESIGN   MINE™

6 |
EVENT   Summer Splash
CLIENT   Renaissance Communications
DESIGN   3rd Edge Communications

Northwest Film and Video Festival

PLAZM

1995 NW Fest judged by programmer John Cooper, start showing up in Park C

1975 NW Fest opens eligibility to B.C. entries, arrogantly declaring southwest Canadians "northwest" filmmakers. Nobody calls us on it.

1989 Longtime festival contributor Jim Blashfield nominated for MTV award for Michael Jackson's *Leave Me Alone*. By 2003, people finally have.

1974 Festival judge rejects Bob Gardiner and Will Vinton's animated short, *Closed Mondays*. Later that year it wins an Oscar.

1976 Taking full advantage of the new rule, Vancouver's Philip Borsos wins Best Documentary. Later directs *The Grey Fox* and judges 14th NW Fest.

1990 Portland reaches apex of grunge cool. Heroin returns to filmmaking.

1999 Final Cut Pro™ comes out. Suddenly everybody's a filmm

1992 Beloved festival contributor Joan Gratz's *Mona Lisa Descending a Staircase* wins Oscar. Joan Collins wears same dress to ceremonies.

1999 Matt Groening judges 26th festival, promises audience, "won't get a splitting headache or a sore ass."

2000 Todd Haynes judges 27th festival. Two years later, *Far From Heaven* nominated for four Oscars. Coincidence?

2002 More than 400 filmmakers vie for the NW Fest screen. 43 make it in. Feelings are hurt. We are officially prestigious.

▷26th annual northwest film and video festival
November 5–12 1999 The Guild Theatre

HARVESTING THE BEST OF THE NORTHWEST

30TH ANNUAL NORTHWEST FILM & VIDEO FESTIVAL
NOVEMBER 6–15 WWW.NWFILM.ORG

The Northwest Arts Center is "a regional media arts resource… founded to encourage the study, appreciation, and utilization of the moving image arts, foster their artistic and professional excellence, and to help create a climate in which they may flourish.

To this end, the center created the annual Northwest Film and Video Festival in Portland, Oregon. Now in its thirty-fourth year, the event brings together leading professionals in the film industry with up-and-coming independent filmmakers living in the Northwest United States and British Columbia, Canada. The goal of this festival is to give voice to original, creative filmmaking outside of the Hollywood machine, and more specifically, to the local filmmaking body with an audience of local moviegoers.

A great deal of the character of this film festival was established by evoking elements of northwest culture. Since 1999, Portland design firm Plazm chose imagery pertaining to either film or the geographic region for its designs for one-sheet posters, trailers, advertisements, T-shirts, tickets, programs, and theater slides for the festival.

Plazm began working with the festival in its twenty-sixth year, creating a poster showing twenty–six individual theater seats, each with a slightly different style, showing the evolution in seating design over the festival's twenty–six year run, a departure from the expected film festival imagery of film canisters, negative reels, or cameras.

The following year, Plazm designed a series of posters, each depicting a stylized, one-color illustration of a different northwest filmmaker accompanied by a quote about their work. The next year, Plazm designed a poster that re-created multicolored television test pattern cards, perhaps to speak to the fact that this festival is not only about filmmakers, but also incorporates artists who shoot on video.

Using a photographic approach, the twenty–ninth annual Northwest Film Festival poster manipulated the verbiage of a Forest Service sign that might be found in the middle of one of the northwest's lush, beautiful forests. The wit and simplicity of Plazm's design lent itself perfectly to other media and was adapted for use on a T-shirt, provided the location for a television ad, and inspired the trees and other foliage used to decorate the opening night party. They tried, although unsuccessfully, to get the Forest Service to make them an actual sign for the event.

For the thirtieth anniversary poster, Plazm used an illustration of a tree stump with its many rings exposed as a metaphorical timeline for the life of the festival, marking significant moments in the history of the festival and filmmaking in general. With both sincerity and a sense of humor, they pointed out such milestones as: the inaugural year of the festival; the year they rejected a film that later won an Academy Award; the year they opened the submissions criteria

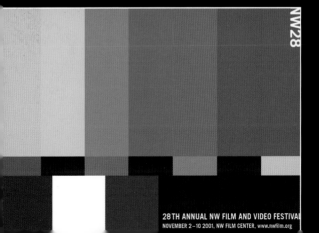

28TH ANNUAL NW FILM AND VIDEO FESTIVAL
NOVEMBER 2–10 2001, NW FILM CENTER, www.nwfilm.org

to include British Columbia; and the year that Final Cut Pro was released, making everyone a "filmmaker." Part of the beauty and character of this particular poster was that it very easily and simply showed the character of the Northwest Film Festival and its supporters.

Plazm has married the goals and personality of the Northwest Film Festival so simply and astutely that, year after year, they are able to design pieces that are both eye-catching and suited to the event they promote. They have perfectly illustrated the goals of the film festival: to give voice to independent filmmaking that is distinctly northwestern

1 | 2 | 3 | 4 | 5 | 6 | 7 | 8 | 9 | 10 | 11 |

EVENT   Revelation Generation Music Festival

CLIENT   Revelation Generation Music Festival

DESIGN   3rd Edge Communications

1

2

3

4

5

6

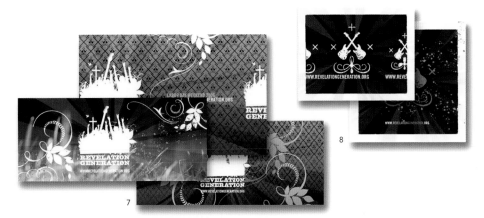

7

8

11

9

10

1 | 2 | 3 | 4 | 5 |

EVENT   Kung-Fu on Belgrade Summer Festival
CLIENT   Belgrade Summer Festival
DESIGN   B92

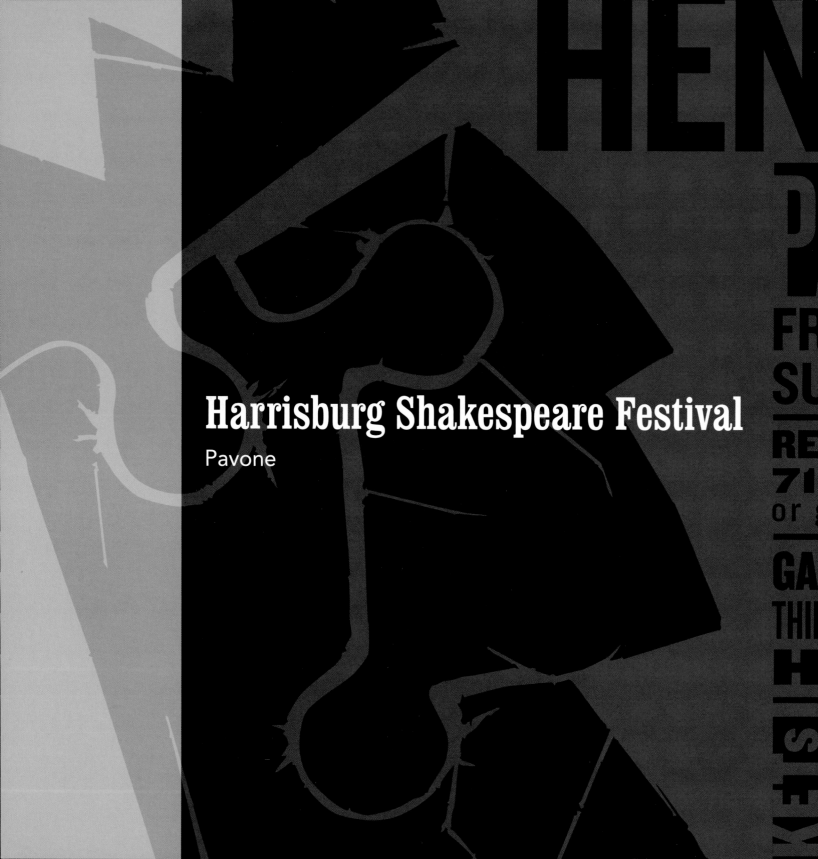

Harrisburg Shakespeare Festival

Pavone

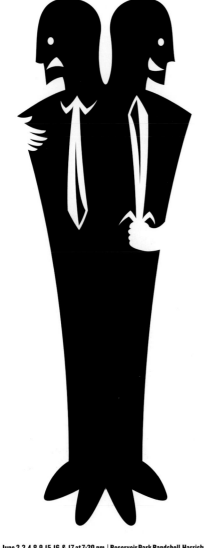

2 Gentlemen of Verona

The Harrisburg Shakespeare Festival (HSF) began in 1994 when the city of Harrisburg, Pennsylvania, was looking to enhance the culture of the region.

Originally conceived as a free summer event to be held in a public park, the success of the festival led to another indoor performance in the fall. The very successful biannual event has had over 39,000 attendees over the near decade and a half since it started and continues to grow as a popular city event.

For the last ten years, Pavone, a Harrisburg, Pennsylvania–based advertising and graphic design firm, has donated its services to the nonprofit HSF. In order to promote community arts outreach, Pavone agreed to develop the HSF identity and produce various promotional materials, including posters, flyers, postcards, T-shirts, buttons, programs, and outdoor advertising. They also created a set of note cards containing artwork and posters from previous shows to sell at the performances to raise additional funds.

Several factors have led to the design aesthetic that Pavone developed for HSF. The fact that HSF is a nonprofit has had a great impact on the design process and has set the tone and strategy for all of the branding

OCT 29 - NOV 22

HENRY IV
PARTS I & II

FRIs & SATs 7:30PM
SUNs 2:30PM
RESERVATIONS:
717-238-4111
or gamutplays.org

STUDENT
MATINEES
TUEss
9:30AM

GAMUT CLASSIC THEATRE
THIRD FLOOR, STRAWBERRY SQUARE
HARRISBURG

$20 GENERAL ADMISSION
$15 STUDENTS/SENIORs

B.Y.O.P. SUNDAYs
(BRING YOUR OWN PRICE)
ANY SIZE DONATION BUYS YOUR
ADMISSION TO THE SHOW.

TICKETS

and promotional materials. With an eye toward keeping production costs low, Pavone developed a one-color set of materials that could be easily printed, photocopied, silk-screened, and cut from vinyl. This black-on-white, seemingly simple approach to the design is actually what sets it apart from other theater marketing materials. In a world of bright, saturated color, these posters stand out as a fresh, minimalist approach with a very graphic appeal. With posters mounted on every streetlight and tree in the area, these stark black-and-white posters descend upon the city of Harrisburg and become a part of the city's visual landscape.

The imagery for the posters is developed out of an understanding of the key elements of the play—its characters, themes, and plot. Several months before the production begins, Pavone meets with the play's director to discuss ideas and any special elements or themes that this particular production may contain. This information then gets distilled to a "comprehensive idea that can be portrayed in a single image." Avoiding clichés and obvious symbolism such as crowns makes this job more challenging but also keeps the resulting work fresh and inventive. The development of the image is greatly impacted by the single-color limitation but lends itself to stylistic illustrations that rely heavily on an imaginative use of negative space. This type of illustratio

is subtle but striking and creates a brand identity that is simple, thoughtful, and reinforces the artistic goals of HSF.

Because Pavone has worked with the HSF for so many years, there has been plenty of opportunity for experimentation with the identity and promotional materials. Some of those explorations have included the introduction of color and the creation of a typographic frame to better highlight the imagery. However, time has proven that tried and tested rings true and the core elements of the identity are still the most effective. The ultimate key to the event's success has proven to be the eye-catching black-and-white poster with a line art illustration.

At the onset of each event, Pavone sets out to "capture the essence of the particular show and run it through the filter of the HSF identity." The audience is drawn to the unique one-color line art illustrations— a stark contrast from our oversaturated four-color world. Budget limitations are almost always a consideration, but in this case, they forced the designers to simplify these ideas to their most basic form. This is no easy task and a lesser designer would not have been able to rise to the challenge. Pavone has created a brand identity that is as interesting, attractive, and effective as any project with unlimited resources could be.

1 |
EVENT   True Stories #1
CLIENT   True Stories
DESIGN   Dotzero Design

2 |
EVENT   True Stories #2
CLIENT   True Stories
DESIGN   Dotzero Design

1

2

1

1

2

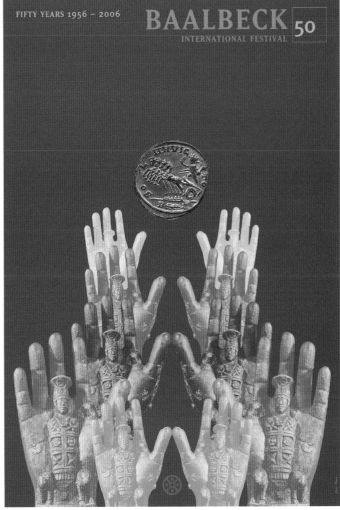

1

stellastarr*
irving plaza new york city
october 6 stellastarr.com

1 |
EVENT   Stellastarr*
CLIENT   Stellastarr* & Sony Music
DESIGN   The Small Stakes

2 |
EVENT   Cabin Fever Film Festival
CLIENT   Trout Unlimited
DESIGN   Dotzero Design

3 |
EVENT   Holocaust and the Moving
          Image Film Festival
CLIENT   BGSU German
          Language Department
DESIGN   Todd Childers Graphic Design

2

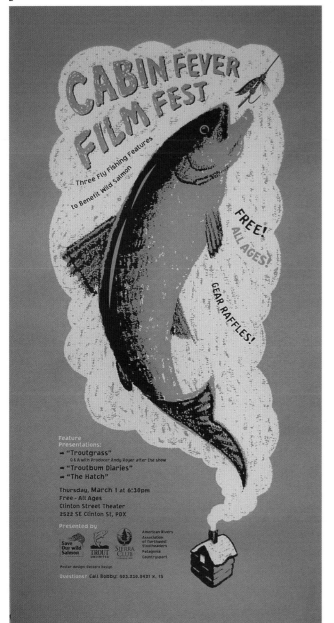

3

the Holocaust and the Moving Image

A public series of lectures, films, and
discussions at **Bowling Green State University**
March-April 2004

The Holocaust and the Moving Image
will open a rare connection between film
and Holocaust scholars and a broader
public. Audiences will have the opportunity
to debate questions of consciousness,
responsibility, art and experience as they
relate to the Holocaust film.

Time/Place
Events begin with speaker's remarks at **7:00pm**

Location: **Gish Film Theater** in Hanna Hall

Parking will be available on the BGSU campus
in lots **a, e,** and **g**
campus map at http://www.bgsu.edu/map/section7.html

Admission: free

For more info: (419) 372 2268
http://www.bgsu.edu/departments/greal/D_news.htm

Sponsors
Office of the Provost
Department of German, Russian, and East Asian
Languages
Ruth Fajerman Markowicz Holocaust Resource
Center of Greater Toledo

18 March
Jakob der Lügner
(Jakob the Liar)
1975, East Germany, 100 min, director: Frank Beyer

A tale of hope, lies, and survival in the Ghetto
near war's end, based on the novel by German-
Jewish writer Jurek Becker. Compare Columbia
Pictures' 1999 re-make (same title), with
Robin Williams as lead.

*Commentators: Kristie Foell and
Christina Guenther, German program, BGSU*

25 March
Al Tiqu Le B'Shoah
(Don't Touch My Holocaust)
1994, Israel, 140 min, director: Asher Tlalim

Documentary on the Akko Theater Center's
production of a play called *Arbeit Macht Frei.*
The film follows the Israel-based, international
troupe of actors as they meet survivors, learn
from documents, and travel to Europe, wrestling
to understand the lives and events they bring
to the stage.

*Commentator: David Brenner, German and
Jewish Studies programs, Kent State University*

1 April
Schindler's List
1993, USA, 195 min, director: Steven Spielberg

Based on the actual figure of Czech-born
businessman Oskar Schindler, who saved over
1,000 Jews from death during World War II.
Spielberg's film, which won seven Oscars in 1994,
has become the chief point of reference in
discussions of Hollywood and the Holocaust.

*Commentator: Michael Bernard-Donals,
English and Jewish Studies programs,
University of Wisconsin - Madison*

8 April
La Vita è Bella
(Life is Beautiful)
1997, Italy, 122 min, director: Roberto Benigni

Moments of profound sadness and joy mark
this film, which won 1999 academy awards for
best foreign language film and best leading
actor (Benigni). Benigni's use of comedy in his
treatment of the Holocaust has divided audiences,
critics, and scholars.

Commentator: Carlo Celli, Italian program, BGSU

All events are free and open to the public.

Sundance Film Festival

AdamsMorioka, Inc.

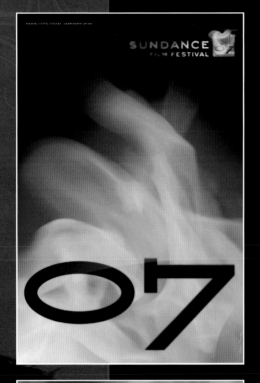

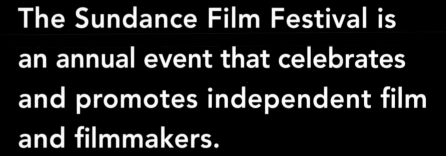

The Sundance Film Festival is an annual event that celebrates and promotes independent film and filmmakers.

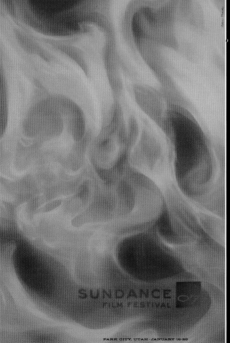

It is the largest independent cinema festival in the United States. Its goal is to increase the value of personal vision in film while promoting it to the entertainment industry and the general public. Having been actively working as part of the larger Sundance family for many years, for the 2007 event, AdamsMorioka handled 150 printed and motion pieces, website visuals, advertising, and environmental graphics for all of Park City, Utah.

Inspiration for the 2007 design arose from a close collaboration with Robert Redford (founder) and Sundance's "eyes," Jan Fleming (producer). "It's hard to say how the "fire" idea came about, but I know that once we moved in that direction, I began to think about those nights camping as a kid in the Sierra Nevadas," recalls Sean Adams, partner and cofounder of AdamsMorioka, Inc.

2005 Sundance Film Festival
Park City, Utah • January 20–30, 2005

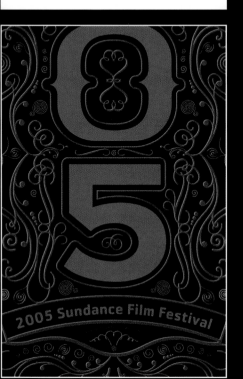

Conceptualizing the design strategy began in April for the festival that launches in January of the following year. The audience for the event consists of several groups: the creative makers, the actual filmmakers, actors, crew, and production individuals who make the films; the industry insiders, people who work in the entertainment business; the "armchair creatives," people who enjoy independent film, museums, art galleries, but are not part of the entertainment industry; and finally, the media, newspapers, websites, and television programs.

It is a challenge and a priority for AdamsMorioka to make sure the message of the Sundance festival does not get lost in all the hype; personal creative vision must trump any superfluous celebrity attention. This is accomplished by making sure each festival year stands on its own and reflects an independent, artistic mindset rather than a mass-culture trend. Sean Adams explains that, "The event is already getting enough attention, if not too much. We work to make sure that the message of independent vision is made clear to all of the media venues that cover the event."

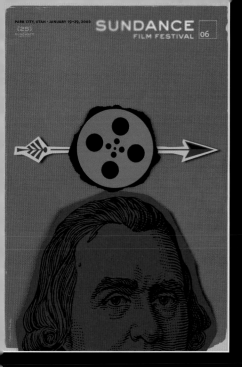

SUNDANCE
FILM FESTIVAL

PARK CITY
UTAH

JANUARY 15-25, 2004

1

2

A Celebration of Movies, Music, and Food

A PREVIEW OF
LETTERMAN DIGITAL ARTS CENTER
One Letterman Drive
The Presidio, San Francisco

JUNE 25TH 2005
Picnic Lunch – Eleven O'Clock
Entertainment – Noon until two

1 | 2 |

EVENT   Letterman Digital Arts Center
         Opening Celebration

CLIENT   Lucasfilm

DESIGN   Elixir Design

1 |

EVENT Pebble Beach
Conours d'Elegance

CLIENT Bombardier Flexjet

DESIGN Greteman Group

2 |

EVENT Downing Concert Series:
Chicago in Concert

CLIENT Wichita Center for the Arts

DESIGN Greteman Group

1 │
EVENT   Entourage Premier
CLIENT   HBO
DESIGN   Tornado Design

1

EVENT   Summer Splash
CLIENT   Renaissance Communications
DESIGN   3rd Edge Communications

1

EVENT   Beach Fest
CLIENT   Massive Radio
DESIGN   Rome & Gold Creative

V Festival

Autumn:01

In 2007, after twelve years in the U.K., Virgin brought its wildly successful V Festival to Australia, hoping to make the inaugural event not just a great concert, but a music experience that would raise the bar for popular music festivals in Australia.

By bringing together some of the best musical acts from around the globe along with local Australian talent, featuring Beck, the Pixies, Pet Shop Boys, Gnarls Barkley, Groove Armada, Bang Gang Deejays, among others, the festival sought to create a once-in-a-lifetime festival experience that was uniquely Australian.

Modular Touring was enlisted to create an unforgettable concert. They, in turn, hired Autumn:01 design firm to create an atmosphere that was vibrant, hip, and unique. To do this, Autumn:01 and art director Kate Kendall wanted to create a brand identity for the event that could be

WORKER

WORKER

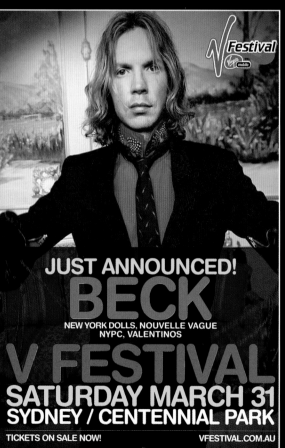

JUST ANNOUNCED!
BECK
NEW YORK DOLLS, NOUVELLE VAGUE
NYPC, VALENTINOS
V FESTIVAL
SATURDAY MARCH 31
SYDNEY / CENTENNIAL PARK
TICKETS ON SALE NOW!   VFESTIVAL.COM.AU

applied through all materials produced, could be built upon in future festivals, and would distinguish Australia's V Festival from its predecessor in the U.K. and other music festivals already taking place in Australia. They also wanted to "imprint a lasting visual memory" and "have strong brand recognition in the lead up to, and after, the event." As such, they chose to take a three-pronged approach to the design, focusing on color, typography, and iconic imagery to create the over-arching brand identity.

By using a CMYK color scheme and modern, bold font, they were able to create a look that was young, hip, energetic, and captures the feeling of excitement surrounding such a large, groundbreaking event. They also chose a number of images that mirrored the iconic nature of the festival. Using a photo of a hand making the universal peace sign, which also looks like a *V* to represent the V Festival, they were able to brand the event in a way that is already familiar to the large viewing audience. The strength of using images of cassette tapes, headphones, and a boom box to brand the individual stages is that they at once represented music and nostalgia, reflecting some of the older and reunited bands that performed and that will continue to be cultivated as the festival goes on each year.

The project began long before the festival itself took place. The print campaign began with a launch party, street, and print advertising, and continued with posters, and postcards. Autumn:01 designed the event website, HTML emails, and created an online viral campaign. At the festival, they designed the look and branding of three stages, directional towers, site maps, information flyers, drink cards, staff clothing and badges, and wristbands. They also created various merchandising products including several styles of T-shirts, drink holders, and beach balls.

In designing such a vast array of materials for such a large event, Autumn:01 was faced with a number of challenges. First, the design studio was brought into the process after it had already begun working with a different design firm. Starting over from scratch and already a bit late in the game, made for extremely tight deadlines. Also, as with any project of this magnitude, they were subject to approvals from various sources including their client, Modular Touring, Virgin, and the various sponsors.

It was important to Autumn:01 to include all of the required advertising without overloading the audience with corporate messages and imagery as other festivals had done, so that the festival experience not

become a commercial experience. This was especially difficult as the Virgin logo had to be present in each piece.

Another design challenge came in the early concepting phases when they were designing the individual stages. Each of the three stage designs had to have equal importance because no one band was headlining the event—every band was considered equal and the stage designs needed to reflect that. So the design team devised a scheme that was cool and consistent across the board.

Through a true understanding of its client, subject, and demographic, Autumn:01 was able to design a festival experience that hit the mark on every level. By using vibrant colors, modern typography, and iconic imagery, they were able to cater to and capture the attention of the youthful demographic of the V Festival. In so doing, they also laid the foundation for a strong, memorable brand identity that could be easily built upon and referenced as this burgeoning festival continued to grow each year.

AFFILIATE

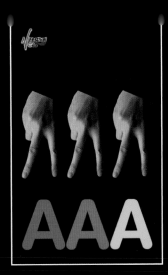

AAA

ARTIST

WORKER

AFFILIATE

PRIVATE PARTIES

1

EVENT   Kimberly and Ryan Getting Hitched
CLIENT   Kimberly Reynolds & Ryan Kelly
DESIGN   D*LSH Design

2

EVENT   Howe Family Reunion
CLIENT   Howe Family
DESIGN   Element

2

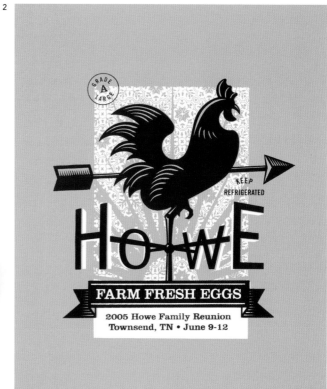

1

1 |
EVENT   McGrath Rogers Wedding
CLIENT   Jennifer McGrath
DESIGN   3

1

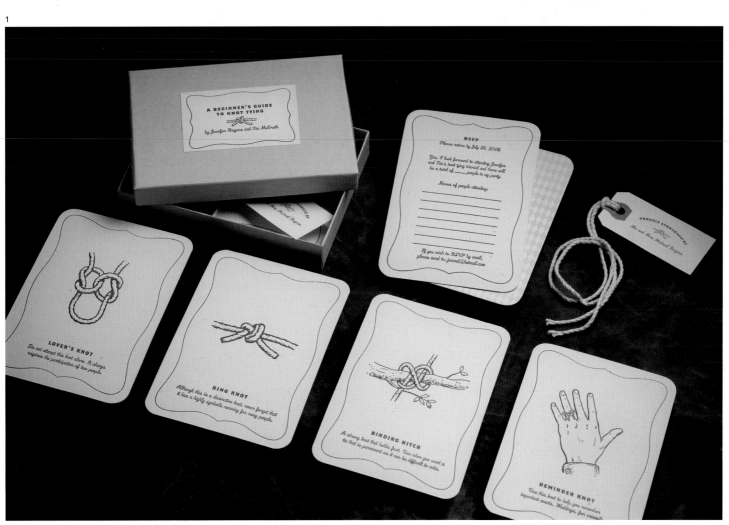

1 |

EVENT   Atkins Wedding
CLIENT   Cheryl & John Atkins
DESIGN   Atkins Design Studio, Inc.

1

1 |
EVENT Jeff Wilt Turns 40
CLIENT Jeff Wilt
DESIGN WORKTODATE

1

1 |

EVENT   Mariana & Daniel Wedding
CLIENT   Mariana Gonzalez
DESIGN   Brown Sugar Design

1 | 2 | 3 | 4 |

EVENT   MM Wedding

CLIENT   MM

DESIGN   Copia Creative, Inc.

1 |
EVENT   Mohatta Wedding
CLIENT   Mohatta
DESIGN   MindsEye Creative

1

1

EVENT   Thirani Wedding
CLIENT   Thirani
DESIGN   MindsEye Creative

1

1

2

1 |
EVENT   McCall / Miller Wedding
CLIENT   McCall / Miller Families
DESIGN   Sunlit Media

2 |
EVENT   Tebbe / Starr Wedding
CLIENT   Shane and Erin Starr
DESIGN   Shane Starr

1 |
EVENT   Houshyar / Westergaard Wedding
CLIENT   Kermit Westergaard
DESIGN   Kermit Westergaard

2 |
EVENT   Nathan's First Birthday
         Hoedown
CLIENT   Thuy Trifunovic
DESIGN   D*LSH Design

1

1 | 2 |
EVENT   Seth's 50th Birthday Party
CLIENT   Rafanelli Events
DESIGN   Fresh Oil

2

1 |

EVENT   Dawn & Edmund's Wedding
CLIENT   Dawn Lai & Edmund Li
DESIGN   Edmund Li

2 |

EVENT   Ceci & Greg's Wedding
CLIENT   Gregory Linsler
DESIGN   UPPERCASE

1

EVENT   Sandoval / Cho Wedding

CLIENT   Yee-Ping Cho

DESIGN   Yee-Ping Cho Design

1

2

1 |
EVENT   Lewis / Peki Wedding
CLIENT   Stacey Lewis and Kostiya Peki
DESIGN   Latrice Graphic Design

2 |
EVENT   Hartje / Lauer Destination Wedding
CLIENT   Shawna Hartje and Todd Lauer
DESIGN   TL Design

1 |
EVENT   Irma's 80th Birthday Soiree
CLIENT   Addison Liquorish
DESIGN   Conversant Studios

1

1

EVENT	Delorefice / Kiri Wedding
CLIENT	Erin Delorefice and Shardul Kiri
DESIGN	UNIT Design Collective

1 |
EVENT   Encinias / Duncan Wedding
CLIENT   The Duncan's
DESIGN   Rome and Gold Creative

1 | 2 | 3 | 4 | 5 | 6 | 7 | 8 | 9 |

EVENT   Danish Advertising
             Awards "Gold Korn"
CLIENT   Creative Circle
DESIGN   Brandcentral

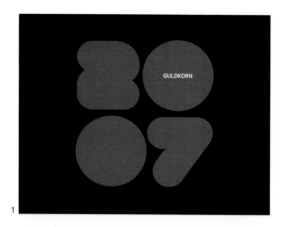

1

4

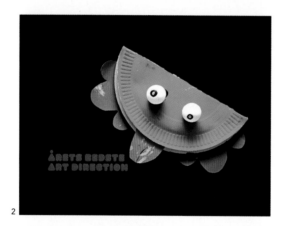

2

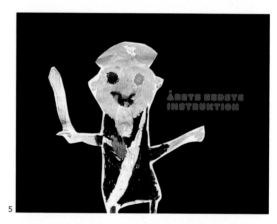

5

3

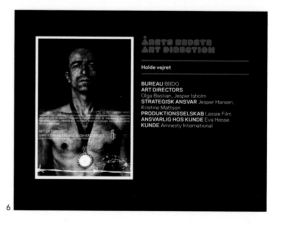

6

Creative Circle præsenterer:

GULDKORN 2007

EFTERFEST
Lørdag den 24. marts kl. 22
på Østre Gasværk,
Nyborggade 17,
Østerbro

underskrift: nummer:

Tøjdyr: Zelda von Wieding Lidin

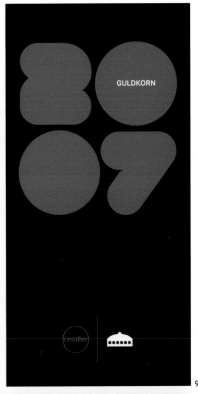

GULDKORN

creative

7

9

KREATIVITETEN LÆNGE LEVE!

Lørdag den 24. marts slår vi dørene op for årets Guldkorn og du er inviteret. Igen i år hylder vi de mest kreative, begavede, nyskabende og imponerende ideer. Niveauet er højt og forventningerne store. Creative Circle vil gerne se dig på Østre Gasværk, Nyborggade 17, Østerbro klokken 17. Skynd dig at bestille billet på camilla@creativecircle.dk - det er trist at stå udenfor

Billetpriser.
Creative Circle medlemmer   1.050 kr.
Ikke Creative Circle medlemmer   1.395 kr.
Efterfest (fra kl. 22):   450 kr.
Alle priser er inkl. moms.

8

2

1 |

EVENT   Imagination Takes Flight:
         Athena Pinnacle Awards

CLIENT   Athena

DESIGN   Incitrio design{brand}media

2 |

EVENT   Awards of Excellence

CLIENT   Bright Horizons

DESIGN   Stoltze Design

1

1

COOLIDGE AWARD

2004
RECIPIENT:

Zhang Yimou, Director
Foreign Language Film

AWARD
COMMITTEE:

Clinton McClung
Elizabeth Taylor-Mead
Connie White
Joe Zina

AWARD
ADVISORY
PANEL:

John Anderson
Ted Barron
Charles Rowan Beye
Sasha Berman
Amy Geller
John Gianvito
Michal Goldman
May Haduong
Marianne Lampke
Rikk Larsen
Marian Masone
Michele Meek
Kathleen Mullen
Lisa Viola
Kaj Wilson

290 HARVARD STREET, BROOKLINE, MASSACHUSETTS 02446 *Telephone:* (617) 734-2501 *Facsimile:* (617) 734-6288 WWW.COOLIDGE.ORG

COOLIDGE CORNER THEATRE FOUNDATION, INC.

1 | 2 |
EVENT   The Coolidge Awards 2004
CLIENT   Coolidge Corner Theatre
DESIGN   Stoltze Design

2

1 |
EVENT   The Coolidge Awards 2006
CLIENT   Coolidge Corner Theatre
DESIGN   Stoltze Design

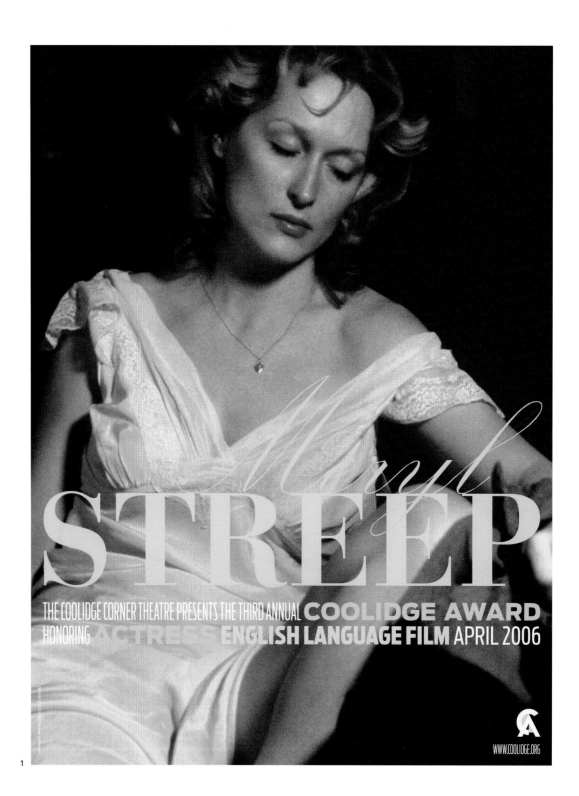

1

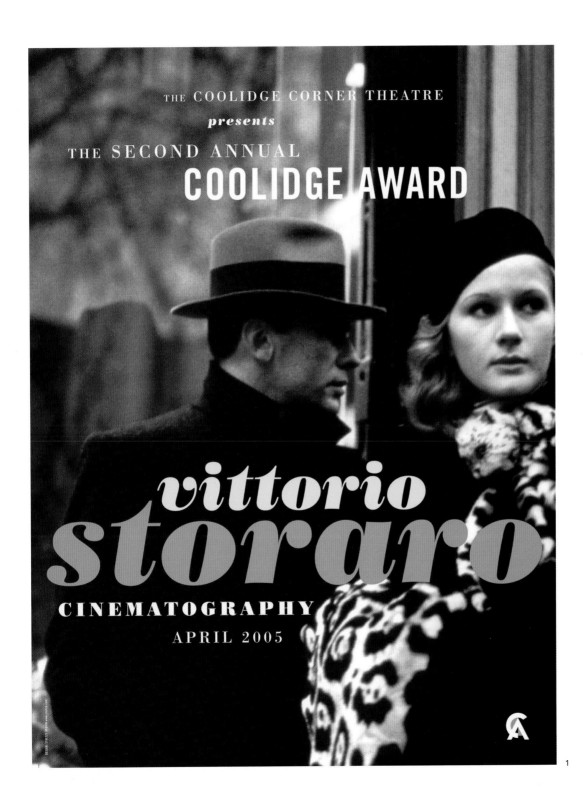

THE COOLIDGE CORNER THEATRE

presents

THE SECOND ANNUAL

COOLIDGE AWARD

vittorio
storaro

CINEMATOGRAPHY

APRIL 2005

1 |
EVENT   The Coolidge Awards 2005
CLIENT   Coolidge Corner Theatre
DESIGN   Stoltze Design

1

1 | 2 | 3 |

EVENT   2006 Baltimore ADDY Awards

CLIENT   Advertising Association
           of Baltimore

DESIGN   substance151

1

2

3

1 | 2 | 3 |

EVENT   2005 Ft. Lauderdale
         ADDY Awards

CLIENT   ADFED of Greater
         Ft. Lauderdale

DESIGN   Gouthier Design, INC.

1

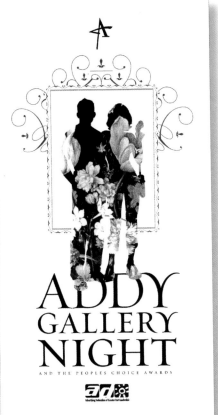

2

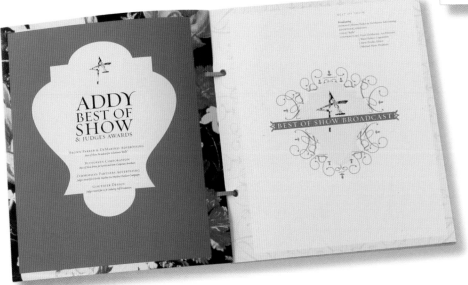

3

1 |
EVENT   2007 ADDY Awards
CLIENT   2007 ADDY Awards
DESIGN   Trilix Marketing Group

1

1

EVENT   The Coolidge Awards 2004
CLIENT   Coolidge Corner Theatre
DESIGN   Stoltze Design

1

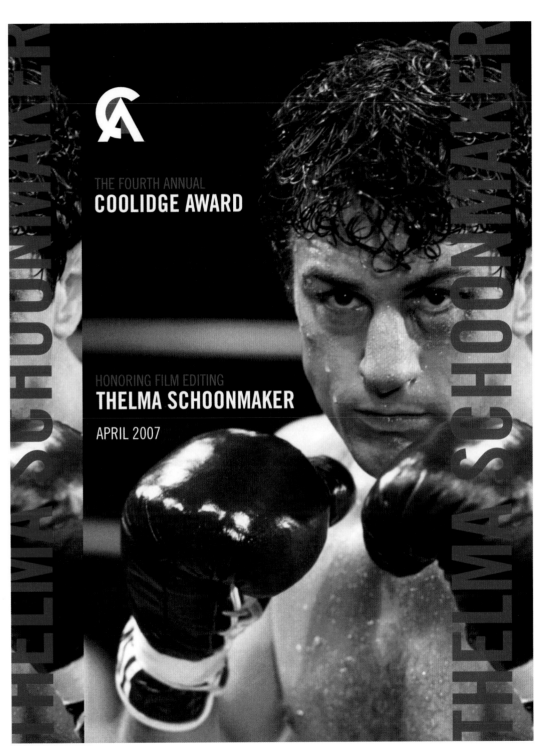

THE FOURTH ANNUAL
COOLIDGE AWARD

HONORING FILM EDITING
THELMA SCHOONMAKER

APRIL 2007

1

EVENT   The Coolidge Awards 2007
CLIENT   Coolidge Corner Theatre
DESIGN   Stoltze Design

1

1

1

EVENT   James Beard
         Foundation Awards

CLIENT   James Beard Foundation

DESIGN   John Kneapler Design

1

1 | 2 | 3 |

EVENT   The HR Excel Awards
CLIENT   Royal Bank of Scotland
DESIGN Traffic Design Consultants

3

 SPORTS & AUTOMOTIVE

1

2

3

4

5

1 | 2 | 3 | 4 | 5 | 6 |
EVENT   This Way to Nike Beautiful
CLIENT   Nike
DESIGN   PLAZM

6

The 2006 NCAA Final Four

Dean Johnson Design

Each March, the NCAA Men's Division I Basketball Championship dominates the sports world for a month-long series of single-elimination playoff games known as March Madness.

This extremely competitive, high-intensity series comes down to the semifinals, called the Final Four, in which the champions of each of the four playoff divisions compete against one another for the prestigious championship spot. In 2006, the Final Four was held at the RCA Dome in Indianapolis to a crowd of nearly 44,000 eager basketball fans per game. The home viewership of this tournament has grown steadily over the years to rival that of any premier sport championship including the Super Bowl, World Series, and NBA finals.

Dean Johnson Design of Indianapolis, Indiana, was hired to design the identity for this high-profile event, which posed many challenges. First, it was to be seen by millions of people across all demographic barriers and would need to have broad appeal. Secondly, the logo would be used as the foundation of the identity for the tournament and would have a wide variety of applications. The logo would need

to work as a full- or one-color image and had to be legible when shrunk down to 1 inch or blown up to 20 feet. The designers also had to contend with the fact that the logo would be applied to a variety of materials and surfaces from embroidery on hats, silk-screening on T-shirts, vinyl, mesh, window decals, foam core, as well as on-screen television graphics. A close eye was kept on production of all of these materials to ensure the colors would stay true across all mediums. The designers also needed to consider and honor the event's locale whenever possible. Finally, they would have to create the proper hierarchy of information within the logo while still including all of the necessary information and the newly redesigned NCAA logo.

DJD created a symbol that represented a sense of speed and motion that was true the game of basketball but was also inspired by Indiana's famed Indy 500 car race. It was important that a limited number of graphic elements, colors, and fonts were used so they could be applied consistently across the huge variety of applications. The logo proved so successful that the NCAA decided to use the Final Four moniker and blue disk in all future Final Four logos as a means of maintaining consistency and building brand equity.

DJD also created a graphics standard for partners and sponsors who would use the identity for merchandising, advertising, and signage that appeared throughout Indianapolis and the arena. This included designing the basketball court floor, arena signage (table

banners, courtside chairs, scoreboard, upper level banners, and signage used to dress the interior of the arena), programs and tickets, exterior signage of the arena (entrances, column wraps, window clings), street pole banners, covered crosswalk signage, hotel signage (entrances, column wraps, window clings) and airport signage (entrances, column wraps, window clings). It was important to maintain the same level of clean simplicity across each design, no matter what materials it would be applied to.

The resulting design focused around the event logo supported by simple graphic elements symbolizing rays of light, motion, and silhouettes of basketball players in motion. These graphics were set against a backdrop of blues, reds, and oranges that complement the similar colors found in the logo itself, creating a sense of excitement that is key to any sporting event.

In approximately eighteen months, Dean Johnson Design created a look and feel for one of the nation's largest sporting events, incorporating all of the energy and excitement needed for such an event, but did so in a way that would be easily applicable across a wide array of different printing techniques and materials. It was a difficult task that was pulled off with relative ease and left the average viewer none the wiser.

1 |
EVENT   Ferrari Festival
CLIENT   Highland Village
DESIGN   Laura Smith Illustration

2 |
EVENT   2000 World Series
CLIENT   Major League Baseball
DESIGN   Laura Smith Illustration

2

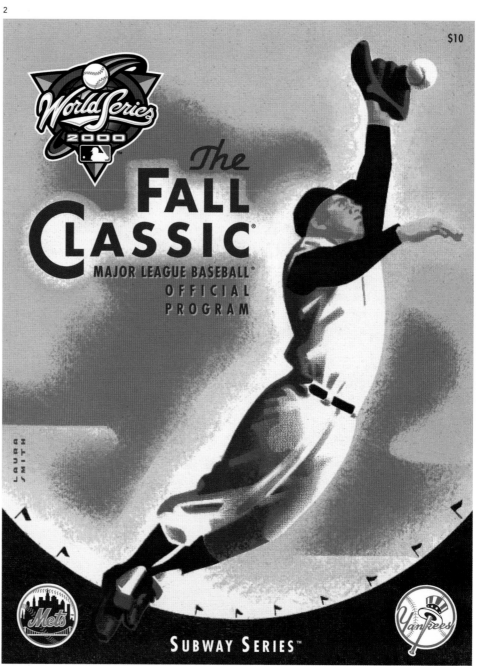

1

1 | 2 |
EVENT The Kentucky Derby
CLIENT Churchill Downs
DESIGN Laura Samith Illustration

1

2

GRANDPRIX
ARIZONA™

3

4

PIPELINE
EAST HAMPTON

PRESENTS

THE FIRST ANNUAL SURF SEMINAR

Free Event
Pro-surfers Teaching World-Class Techniques
Everyone 13–20 Yrs Old
Beginner To Experienced
Free Boards Available / Free Refreshments
Co-Sponsored By Christian Surfers US

MAIN BEACH
EAST HAMPTON

Saturday, Sept 23rd   9am–Noon

5

1 |
EVENT   Sisters Rodeo
CLIENT   Sisters Rodeo Association
DESIGN   Jeff Fisher LogoMotives

2 |
EVENT   Junior Olympic Games
CLIENT   Junior Olympic Games
DESIGN   Sayles Graphic Design

3 |
EVENT   Grand Prix Arizona
CLIENT   Grand Prix Arizona
DESIGN   Campbell Fisher Design

4 |
EVENT   Eugene Marathon
CLIENT   Eugene Marathon
DESIGN   Kendall Ross

5 |
EVENT   1st Annual Surf Seminar
CLIENT   Pipeline
DESIGN   3rd Edge Communication

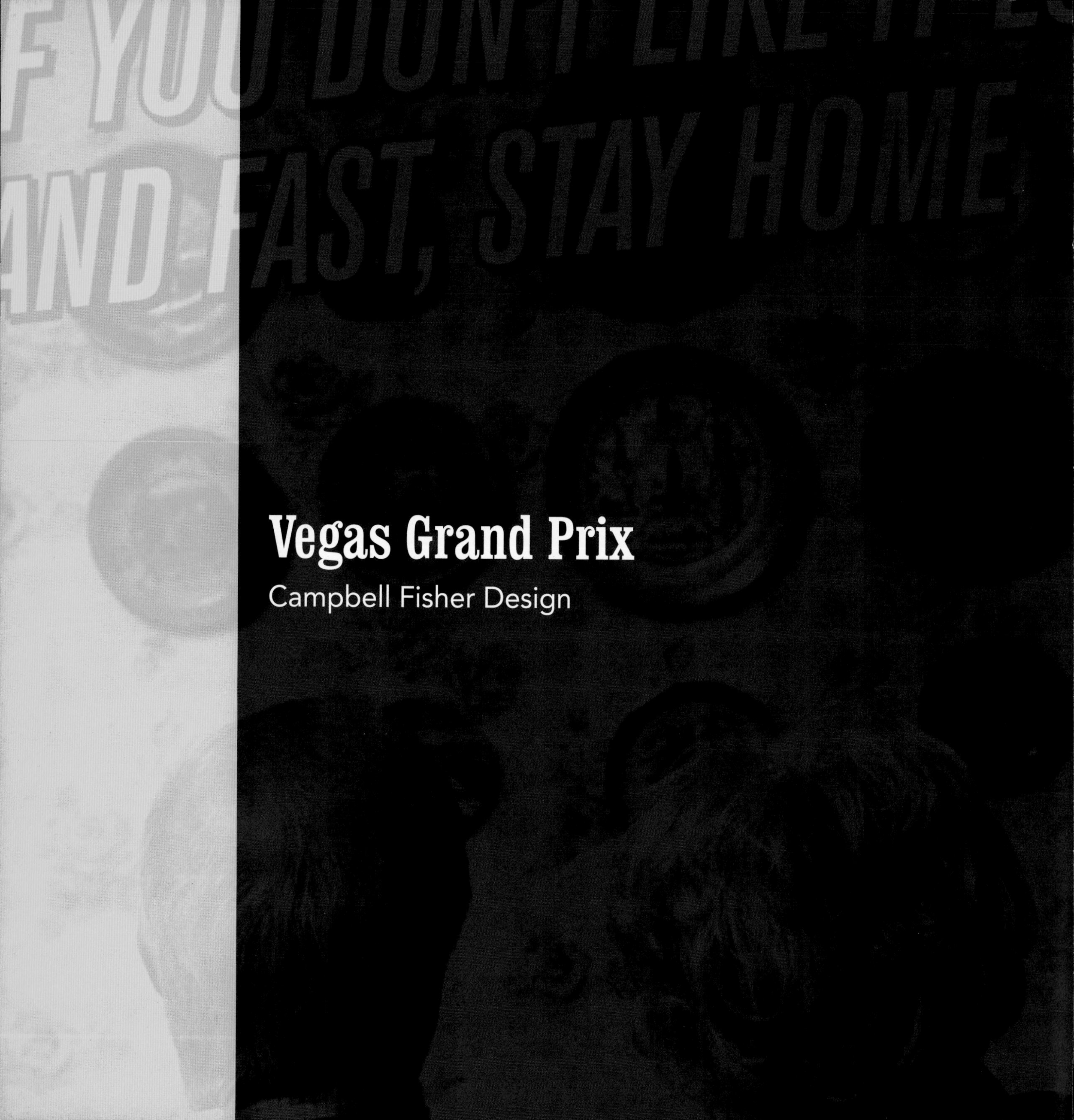

Vegas Grand Prix

Campbell Fisher Design

IT'S NOT YOUR DADDY'S HOT LAP

GET YOUR PASS TO OUR THREE-DAY FESTIVAL OF SPEED.
APRIL 6-8, 2007   WWW.VEGASGRANDPRIX.COM.
CHAMP CAR

VEGAS GRAND PRIX

IF YOU DON'T LIKE IT LOUD AND FAST, STAY HOME

GET YOUR PASS TO OUR THREE-DAY FESTIVAL OF SPEED.
APRIL 6-8, 2007   WWW.VEGASGRANDPRIX.COM
CHAMP CAR

VEGAS GRAND PRIX

In true Las Vegas fashion, the Vegas Grand Prix partnered with Champ Car to bring grand prix racing back to Las Vegas with a no-holds-barred, sexy, decadent, and thrilling three-day festival of speed and entertainment.

The event attracted racing fans and affluent visitors from around the world, generating $76 million dollars for the Las Vegas economy. The festival incorporated open wheel racing, superstar concert events, extreme sports demonstrations, a celebrity poker tournament, and a charity gala to create an array of events each as exciting and enticing as the last. Because of the various activities, it attracted a variety of people including enthusiasts of racing, music, and extreme sports, as well as Las Vegas tourists who happened to be there at the time.

When Campbell Fisher Design (CFD) launched into the design of this event, it recognized the need to establish an exciting, memorable brand, and a complete marketing campaign that was long-term, recognizable, and one with which the audience could easily identify. The campaign needed to convey the image of the event as "fast, fun and sexy." The inspiration for the design came from the vibrancy, energy and excess of Las Vegas itself. CFD used sexy imagery, illustrations, color, and copywriting to create a brand that was risqué and exerted high energy.

The scope of the project was quite large and included a brand identity, website, promotional videos, TV, radio, and print advertising, sponsorship brochures, billboards (both moving and LED), vehicle graphics, greeting cards, apparel, posters, tickets, charity gala invitations, street banners, and retail merchandise. To create a cohesive brand identity across the vast campaign elements, CFD needed to hone in on the most important aspects of the event branding. The theme of the events came down to three main points: glitz, glamour, and glory. Incorporating these three ideas with the energy of the fast, fun, and sexy motifs brought the design to a place that was exciting, and fun, sophisticated, and seductive.

Setting the tone for the whole campaign, CFD developed a bright red logo with imagery of stylized wings and modern, sleek typography. The bold red mark is forceful and sexy, stands out no matter what is behind it, and serves as a perfect unifying element across various pieces of the collateral and advertising. In fact, much of this advertising embodies the same elements that make this logo so strong. This series of print advertising incorporates the same striking red across the bottom of the page beneath a risqué photograph and taglines that seeks to appeal to the reader's wild side. The graphics alone make a bold statement, but it is the tagline that takes the message to the next level, stating that the Vegas Grand Prix is just what the viewer needs to inject some scintillation and excitement into their lives. The taglines include "Start your day off a little racier," "Our back ends

come with spoilers," "Not your daddy's hot lap," and "If you don't like it loud and fast, stay home." This copywriting also gave life to the posters that CFD developed as part of the larger campaign. The simple but clever phrases pair perfectly with the already bold and iconic imagery, allowing the pieces to go from merely interesting to engaging and exciting.

The invitation to the charity gala event used these elements as well, but did so in a way that was elegant, attractive, stylish, and understated. The benefit, which kicked off the Grand Prix event week, was to raise money for the Jenyon Foundation and the Foundation for the Lou Ruvo Brain Institute, a Las Vegas organization fighting Alzheimer's, Parkinson's, Huntington's, ALS, and memory disorders. The clean, white invitation folio was accented with striking red cards and a CD textured to feel like a record. The CD featured music from Jon Bon Jovi and Big and Rich, two of the event's performers. It also featured an embossed, modified starburst shape that alluded to the energy and excitement of the larger event, but did so in a reserved and sophisticated way. This tactile piece added dimension to the whole and showed how the design could be adapted to a more sophisticated piece. The fact that CFD took a brand identity and successfully applied it in ways that was at times decadent and scintillating and at other times understated and elegant, showed the strength of this campaign.

1 |

EVENT   Team Red Bull Vegas Party

CLIENT   Team Red Bull

DESIGN   Archrival

2 |

EVENT   Sports: Breaking Records,
          Breaking Barriers

CLIENT   Smithsonian Institution

DESIGN   Grafik Marketing Communications

1 | 2 |
EVENT   Junior Olympic Games
CLIENT   Junior Olympic Games
DESIGN   Sayles Graphic Design

1

2

1 |
EVENT   Nike: The Ambassadors
CLIENT   Nike
DESIGN   PLAZM

1 |
EVENT   Nike: Heritage Basketball
CLIENT   Nike
DESIGN   PLAZM

1

The National Collegiate
Rock Paper Scissors Tournament

Archrival

of America holds the National Collegiate Rock Paper Scissors Tournament.

Competitions are held in as many as 500 campuses across the United States, the winners of which win a free trip for themselves and one trainer to participate in the national tournament. The 2006 championship tournament was held in New York's famed Madison Square Garden. While the main goal of the tournament was to identify the national collegiate champion, the secondary goal was to make sure that every participant and viewer had a great time so that the participants will return to their campuses as heroes, touting the praises of the tournament and College Bookstores of America.

Archrival in Lincoln, Nebraska, took on the challenge of conceptualizing and designing this event. While there is, as Archrival states, a "quiet humor" to the event, it is mostly branded as a serious, competitive, athletic event. Each competitor is referred to as an "athlete" who has a trainer and is competing for a national championship honor. To that end, Archrival decided to brand this as an athletic event. To market the tournament, they designed three different posters, billboards, buttons, and viral, and marketing materials for individual college competitions. For the event itself, Archrival designed posters,

banners, referee uniforms, medals, trophies, motion graphics, and various other event materials. The competition took place in a ring that was adorned with banners and huge TVs that displayed the bios and stats of each competitor. The athletes who made it to the final rounds wore medals also designed by Archrival.

Archrival had to create a design concept that would find the delicate balance between giving voice to the humor inherent to a rock-paper-scissors tournament and the serious nature of the championship. Each of the three posters firmly established a sports theme by branding them with the logo prominently placed in the center and with a hand reaching from beneath it in either of the rock, paper, or scissors formation. The banners, posters, and graphics used in the arena included these elements, but also incorporated imagery of the locale such as the New York City skyline and the Statue of Liberty. Many other pieces, such as buttons, T-shirts, badges, and faux money, also followed these design motifs to help round out the overall branding. The three finalists took home elaborate trophies with a matte metal finish that are adorned with lightning bolts, starbursts, and a closed fist affixed at the top.

The overall look of the materials seems to have drawn inspiration from the sharp edges and clean, bold sans-serif typography of the midcentury modern look of the 1950s and 1960s as well as some military design elements. Movement lines, the lightning bolt, and the starburst design also have a distinctly retro modern sensibility. Both the logo and finalist trophies conjure images of the flight wings and badges of honor worn on old military uniforms.

The National Collegiate Rock Paper Scissors Tournament is as cool and fun as it is serious and competitive. The design matches this sentiment while also creating a hip, retro, and even chic feel.

 DESIGN DIRECTORY

25projects.com
Katy Fischer
25projects.com

3
Tim McGrath
www.whois3.com

3rd Edge Communications
Rob Monroe
www.3rdedge.com

Aaron Preciado Design
Aaron Preciado
aaronap@yahoo.com

Abstract Studio
Benjamin Della Rosa
www.abstractstudio.net

AdamsMorioka, Inc.
Monica Schlaug
www.adamsmorioka.com

Anne Pikkov
pikkov@hot.ee

Another Limited Rebellion
Noah Scalin
www.alrdesign.com

Archrival
Carey Goddard
www.archrival.com

Atkins Design Studio, Inc.
Cheryl Atkins
www.atkinsdesignstudio.com

Autumn:01
Kate Kendall
www.autumn01.com

Azadeh Houshyar
& Kermit Westergaard
www.daisydust.com

B92
Igor Orsolic
www.b92.net

Belyea
Naomi Cox
Nicholas Johnson
www.belyea.com

The Bingham Group, Inc.
Lisa Bingham
Roger Greene
www.binghamgroup.com

Bohnsack Design
Chris Bohnsack
www.bohnsackdesign.com

Bowhaus Design Group
Mary Porcelli
www.bowhausdesign.com

Brandcentral
Gerard Whelan
www.brandcentral.dk

Brown Sugar Design
Jonathan Speir
www.bsdstudio.com

C3 - Creative Consumer Concepts
www.c3.to

Calagraphic Design
Ronald J. Cala II
www.ronaldjcala2.com

Campbell Fisher Design
GG LeMere
Eliska Ramirez
Kristy Roehrs
www.thinkcfd.com

CDI Studios
Tracy Casstevens
Brian Felgar
Aaron Moses
www.cdistudios.com

Chemi Montes Design
Chemi Montes
www.chemimontesdesign.com

Chris Green Design
Chris Green
www.home.earthlink.net/~chrisgreen/

CHSC design
Christoph Schroeer
www.chsc-design.de

cinquino+co.
Ania J. Murray
www.cinquino.com

The Compound Design
Chad Sawyer
www.compounddesign.com

Conversant Studios
Francheska Guerrero
www.conversantstudios.com

Copia Creative, Inc.
www.copiacreative.com

Crystal Dennis
crystal.dennis@realartusa.com

Dale Harris
Dale Harris
www.daleharris.com

David Clark Design
Roger Beerworth
David Clark
Scott Dawson
Becky Gelder
www.davidclarkdesign.com

The Design Studio
at Kean University
Steven Brower
www.stevenbrowerdesign.com

DISTINC
Jean-Marc Durviaux
John Wiese
www.distinc.net

D*LSH Design
Lucia Dinh
Henny Setiadi
www.dlshdesign.com

Dotzero Design
Jon Wippich
www.dotzerodesign.com

Edmund Li
Edmund Li
edmund.li@sympatico.ca

elaine inspired
Elaine Chernov
www.elaineinspired.com

Element
Jeremy Slagle
www.elementville.com

Elixir Design
Aine Coughlin
Nathan Durrant
Kevin Head
Scott Hesselink
Ashley Hofman
Holly Holmquist
Jennifer Jerde
Sumi Shin
www.elixirdesign.com

Elixirion
Konstantinos Petridis
Michael Sachpazis
www.elixirion.gr

Emma, Inc.
Allison Davis
www.myemma.com

Endless Possibilities Productions, Inc.
Gabrielle Raumberger
www.eposinc.com

Eye Design Studio
Jason Robinson
www.eyedstudio.com

Fabio Ongarato Design
Andrea Wilcock
www.fodesign.com.au

FIDM Publications
Danielle Foushée
www.daniellefoushee.com

Firebelly Design
Dawn Hancock
www.firebellydesign.com

Fragile Design
Naomi Scott
www.fragiledesign.com.au

Fresh Oil
Dan Stebbings
www.freshoil.com

FUNNEL.TV
Eric Kass
www.funnel.tv

gdloft
Allan Espiritu
www.gdloft.com
Gee + Chung Design
Fani Chung
Earl Gee
www.geechungdesign.com

Go Welsh
Nichelle Narcisi
Craig Welsh
www.gowelsh.com

Golden Lasso
Philip Shaw
www.goldenlasso.com

Gouthier Design, Inc.
Jonathan Gouthier
www.gouthier.com

Grafik Marketing Communications
Mila Arrisueno
Gregg Glaviano
Richard Hamilton
David Kasparek
Lynn Murphy
Julie Myers
Johnny Vitorovich
www.grafik.com

Greteman Group
Sonia Greteman
www.gretemangroup.com

HA Design
Handy Atmali
www.creativehotlist.com/h_atmali

Hesselink Design
Scott Hesselink
www.hesselinkdesign.com

HOW
Bryn Mooth
www.howconference.com

Imagine That Design Studio
Patti Mangan
www.imaginethatsf.com

Incitrio design{brand}media
Karen Ong
www.incitrio.com

Innovative Interfaces
Dean Hunsaker
www.iii.com

Jeff Fisher LogoMotives
Jeff Fisher
www.jfisherlogomotives.com

Jenn David Design
Jenn David Connolly
www.jenndavid.com

Jenny Duarte Graphic Design
Jenny Duarte
www.jennyduarte.com

Joe Miller's Company
Joe Miller
www.joemillersco.com

John Kneapler Design
Tony Bartolucci
John Kneapler
Jessica McMaster
www.johnkneaplerdesign.com

The Jones Group
Katherine S. Irvin
Kendra Lively
Chris Lowndes
www.jonesdesign.com

Joven Orozco Design
Joven Orozco
www.jovenville.com

Juicebox Designs
Jay Smith
www.juiceboxdesigns.com

Kate Resnick
Kate Resnick
resnick@american.edu

KBDA
Liz Burril
Keith Knueven
www.kbda.com

Kendall Ross
Sarah Forster
David Kendall
www.kendallross.com

Keyword Design
Judith Mayer
www.keyworddesign.com

Kira Evans Design
Kira Evans
Letitia Rogers
www.kiraevansdesign.com

Kolegram
Gontran Blais
www.kolegram.com

Kradel Design
Maribeth Kradel-Weitzel
kradelm@philau.edu

kristincullendesign
Kristin Cullen
www.kristincullen.com

Latrice Graphic Design
Vicki L. Meloney
vlatrice@comcast.net

Laura Smith Illustration
Laura Smith
www.LauraSmithArt.com

Lloyds Graphic Design Ltd
Alexander Lloyd
lloydgraphics@xtra.co.nz

Marc Posch Design, Inc.
Marc Posch
www.marcposchdesign.com

Matthias Ernstberger Design
Matthias Ernstberger
mernstberger@gmx.de

Messiah College
David Kasparek
www.visualmentalstimuli.com

Michael Doret/Alphabet Soup
Michael Doret
www.MichaelDoret.com

Mindseye Creative
Arati Parikh
Uttara Shah
www.mecstudio.com

MINE
Tim Belonax
Christopher Simmons
www.minesf.com

Morris! communication
Steven Morris
www.thinkmorris.com

Nassar Design
Nelida Nassar
design.nassardesign.com

Nita B. Creative
Renita Breitenbucher
Jessica French
www.nitabcreative.com

Pagliuco Design Company
Maya Bruck
Chad Meyer
Wade Niday
Michael Pagliuco
www.pagliuco.com

Pavone
Robinson Smith
www.pavone.net

PLAZM
Carole Ambauen
Brian Baker
Joshua Berger
Todd Houlette
Drew Marshall
Eric Mast
Pete McCracken
Jon Steinhorst
Wes Youssi
www.plazm.com

POP23
Scott Lahodny
www.pop23.com

Pratt Institute
Arianna Toft
www.pratt.edu

Reactor
Clifton Alexander
Becky Brown
Cody Langford
Chase Wilson
www.yourreactor.com

Real Art Design Group, Inc.
Crystal Dennis
www.realartusa.com

Red Rocket Design & Advertising
Craig Morris
www.redrocket.co.za

RED studios
Ruben Esparza
Rosa Lee
www.redstudios.com

Refinery Design Company
Mike Schmalz
refinery@refinerydesignco.

Rome & Gold Creative
Lorenzo Romero
www.rgcreative.com

S&N Design
Cathy Mores
www.sndesign.net

Sayles Graphic Design
Sheree Clark
John Sayles
www.saylesdesign.com

Schilling Design
Stacy Schilling
www.schilling-design.com

Scorsone / Drueding
Alice Drueding
Joe Scorsone
www.sdposters.com

Seesponge
Michael Bartello
www.seesponge.com

Shane Starr
www.shanestarr.com

SILNT
Felix Ng
www.silnt.com

Silverscape, LLC.
Deirdre Carmichael
www.silverscape.com

The Small Stakes
Jason Munn
www.thesmallstakes.com

Spark! Communications, Inc.
Sherri Lawton
www.spark-communications.com

Stoltze Design
Mary Ross
www.stoltze.com

Stavitsky Design
Vitaly Stavitsky
www.airdesign.ru

**Student Advertising
Graphics Association**
Devin Marra
www.csun.edu/saga

Subplot Design, Inc
Steph Gibson
www.subplot.com

substance151
Ida Cheinman
Rick Salzman
www.substance151.com

Sunlit Media
Erin McCall
www.sunlit-media.com

Synergy Grafix
Remo Strada
www.synergygrafx.com

THERE
Jackie Hawkins
www.there.com.au

Thomson
Yana Slivinsky
www.thomson.com

TL Design
Todd Lauer
www.toddlauerdesign.com

Todd Childers Graphic Design
Todd Childers
www.toddtype.blogspot.com

TOKY Branding+Design
Katy Fischer
Dan Klevorn
Karin Soukup
Geoff Story
Eric Thoelke
www.toky.com

Tom Fowler, Inc.
Elizabeth P. Ball
www.tomfowlerinc.com

Tomato Košir s.p.
Tomato Košir
www.tomatokosir.com

Tornado Design
Al Quattrocchi
Jeff Smith
www.tornadodesign.la

Traffic Design Consultants
Scott Witham
www.traffic-design.co.uk

Tricia Bateman
tricia.bateman@gmail.com

Trilix Marketing Group
Kelly Bittner
Paul Burger
Matt Dirkx
Brent Wirth
www.trilixgroup.com

Turner Duckworth
Shawn Rosenberger
David Turner
www.turnerduckworth.com

Tyler School of Art
Kelly Holohan
www.temple.edu/tyler/gaid.html

UMS Design studio
Ulhas Moses
www.umsdesign.com

UNIT design collective
David Blacker
Jason Botta
Erin Delorefice
Ann Jordan
Shardul Kiri
www.unitcollective.com

UPPERCASE
Omar Mexicano
www.UPPERCASE.com.mx

View Design Company
Deborah Brown
www.viewdesigncompany.com

Wallace Church, Inc.
Jhomy Irrazaba
Maritess Manaluz
Bird Tubman
www.wallacechurch.com

Walsh Associates
Kevin Goodbar
www.walshassoc.com

Wing Chan Design, Inc.
Wing Chan
www.wingchandesign.com

WORKTODATE
Greg Bennett
www.WORKTODATE.com

Yee-Ping Cho Design
Yee-Ping Cho
www.ypcdesign.com

SPECIAL THANKS

To the talented team who helped make this book come to life:

Natalia Naduris-Weissman for her creativity and organization
Shachar Lavi for her style and design
Audra Keefe for her dedication and skills
Marcelo Coelho for his photography
Dave Dresden for his spirit and support
Christina Felix for her efforts and dedication
Emily Potts for her guidance and editing
Regina Grenier for her passion and direction

To the amazing people who have contributed to our success over the years:

Rebekah Albrecht
Katie Anderson
Ilise Benun
Angelia Bibbs-Sanders
Sheri Bonwell
Paul Carlin
Liz Cohen
Tara Curtis
Jim Dekker
Ruben Esparza
Kevin Fabian
Matt Gerbel
Rhonda Glasscock
Joanne Gold
Scott Goldman

Amy Goldsmith
James Grey
Ilene Guy
Terese Harris
Jerri Hemsworth
Ricky Hoyt
Lea Ann Hutter
Louis Katz
Nir Keren
Leah Kim
Lee Lavi
Nina Madjid
Patti Magnan
Gregg McBride
Heather McKendry

Marc McLean
Alexis Mercurio
Bryn Mooth
Steve Morris
Kathy Mota
Michael Page
Tom Parker
Clive Pearse
Doug Prinzivalli
Debbie Reiner
Erin Sarpa
Kat Sawyer
Karen Schakarov
Eva Sippel
Billye Sluyter

Laurence Stevens
Molly Stretten
Healit Swisa
Nativ Top
Reuven Top
Ahuva Top
Mor Top
Deb Valle
Roxana Villa
Dina Weinberg
Rashelle Westcott
Pat Whiteman
Mary Yanish
Jay Zaltzman